THE PHONE EATS FIRST COOKBOOK

Rizzoli
NEW YORK

New York Paris London Milan

THE PHONE EATS FIRST COOKBOOK

50 OF SOCIAL MEDIA'S
BEST RECIPES TO
FEED YOUR FEED . . .
AND THEN YOURSELF

ALLYSON REEDY

FOREWORD BY SNEJANA ANDREEVA
@themodernnonna

PHOTOGRAPHY BY CHELSEA CHORPENNING

To my two little taste testers

CONTENTS

LUNCH
19

& SIDES
45

DRINKS
113

FOREWORD

Snejana Andreeva, @themodernnonna

When I first started sharing recipes and food content online, the Internet was a pretty tame place for debuting your favorite weeknight dinner. You might get a few comments, likes, and re-shares. Fast-forward to the past decade and something wild developed: viral recipes. These are recipes that take the Internet by storm, captivating entire generations, and, in some cases, defining moments in time (I'm looking at you, pandemic dalgona coffee).

So, what is it about butter boards and rice paper dumplings that put people in such a chokehold? Well, the thing about viral recipes is that they're brilliant. They're universally appealing. And sharing the common experience of making them helps connect us. They take ordinary ingredients and transform them into something extraordinary. Hello, Boba Tea Custard Toast (page 9), Cajun Corn Ribs (page 65), and Japanese Soufflé Pancakes (page 5).

They also offer copycats of some of the most beloved restaurant dishes of our time. Of course, I want Carbone's spicy rigatoni at home without the reservation! These viral recipes expose us to new flavors and new methods of meal planning. Chopped Turkey Sandwiches (page 42), Smash Burgers (page 76), lasagna soup—I didn't know what I was missing till I met you!

I'll never forget when my first recipe went viral on TikTok. I couldn't have picked a more meaningful recipe to blow up. My grandmother's no-knead peasant bread: a few humble ingredients easily combined into a dough and baked off until crusty and golden-brown. I shared this bread as a way of honoring my late grandmother, who passed a few months before I posted the recipe. Never in my wildest dreams could I have imagined millions of people around the world making one of the foods I'm most nostalgic about. It was from this experience that I began to appreciate how viral recipes are a way to bring people together.

Home cooks from California to Australia making my *bapche*'s peasant bread? It doesn't get any better than that.

Certain viral recipes just make sense. My Lasagna Soup (which you can find on page 40) is one of them. We all want incredible food with minimal effort, and this soup is just that: all the flavor and satisfaction of a lasagna, without the hassle of making multiple sauces, layering a casserole, and waiting on a long bake time. This soup is comfort in a bowl, and it's easy to see why it's such a beloved and highly shared recipe.

The same can be said of the Jennifer Aniston salad, a recipe I didn't expect to go viral, though it has all the hallmarks of a perfect meal: delicious, satisfying, beautiful, and healthy. When I posted this salad in 2022, I mentioned that it was rumored that Jen ate this every day on the set of *Friends*. When national news stations started to re-share my salad recipe, I knew it was a runaway hit. And even though it has since been debunked that this was Jen's daily lunch (turns out it was actually a Cobb salad, lol!), I can see why the Internet would go nuts for this one: it's the perfect salad to meal-prep and works for so many special diets.

The truth is, I love food trends, but they don't always love me back. The TikTok watermelon and mustard trend nearly had me passing out. That combination? Let's just say it was not for me.

But that's the joy of cooking: discovering new flavors, figuring out what you're obsessed with and what you can live without. Looking for the next 500/10 recipe, your next hyper-fixation meal? You've come to the right place! Allyson weeds out the watermelon-mustard trends, leaving us with only the tastiest recipes that social media has to offer. I hope you have fun making and eating these viral social media recipes. Just remember that the phone eats first.

INTRODUCTION

There are currently more active Instagram users in the world than people who vote, and many of us spend more time on TikTok than with loved ones—so yeah, visual-heavy social media is kind of a thing. And it's not like we're using these apps to show off photos of our unadorned oatmeal or gross-looking chicken breasts.

No, we want the world to think we're eating every color of the rainbow each morning in our smoothie bowls; that our dinner is a sloppy-chic tangle of pasta, fresh basil leaves, and shaved Parmesan; and that we really, truly can turn a piece of toast into a work of art. We want to show our frenemies that not only are we downing Bloody Marys on the reg, but that those Bloodys are topped with bacon, fried chicken, and lobster tails.

The Phone Eats First Cookbook is made for this moment. It's a compilation of only the tastiest, most beautiful Instagram- and TikTok-famous recipes from top food bloggers, chefs, influencers, and recipe creators—#nofilter needed. It includes the recipes that keep popping up in your feed—from new things to do with frozen fruit to specialties from across the globe—and crazily effective techniques like smashing burgers and making sushi in ice cube trays.

Simultaneously celebrating and poking a little fun at our social media–obsessed culture, *The Phone Eats First Cookbook* is an ode to how Instagram and TikTok have affected what we eat, putting foods that many of us in the U.S. had never heard of not only on the digital map but on our physical map as well. Case in point: Birria Tacos (page 71) didn't exist on most menus at Mexican restaurants in the United States until 2018, when L.A. influencers made Instagram stars out of tiny taco trucks slinging glistening, griddled tacos sopping up dark, meaty pools in Styrofoam cups. Have you seen hot chicken or bubble tea spots popping up in your neighborhood? You can thank social media for that. And surveys show that more than one out of three Instagram users have ordered food with no intention of eating it, but just to take a picture of it for their socials.

Besides impacting what we're eating, social media has changed how we let others know that we're feasting on cacio e pepe pasta for dinner. In a way it's the great equalizer, giving an everyday person armed with an iPhone and a TikTok account the ability to create food trends. There's power in social media, and not just in making our exes jealous with beautifully lit bathroom selfies, but in helping others discover new food favorites.

The Phone Eats First Cookbook is also a challenge to the daily social media user: Just try not to eat these tantalizing dishes before first snapping a photo for the 'gram.

Look, it's not like social media is going away or we're getting any less vain as a society, so let's collectively lean into the food porn. Instead of asking why you need a copycat recipe for the Starbucks Pink Drink with chocolate cold foam (page 118), ask why you haven't yet made it and posted it on your socials.

WHO I AM

As a longtime professional restaurant critic and food writer, I've dug through the literally hundreds of millions of food pics and videos on social media to pluck out the best-looking (and, of course, best-tasting) recipes so you, dear reader, don't have to spend hours going down Instagram rabbit holes.

My edit of the Instagram and TikTok overwhelm is focused on the same things I look for when reviewing a restaurant: deliciousness, innovation, welcoming

hospitality (which translates to a welcoming digital personality/account), and, let's be honest, something that looks great on the plate, in the bowl, or, as in the case of some social media crazes, in the muffin tin.

Admittedly, I started out as a social media skeptic—I only got on Instagram when my *Denver Post* editor pretty much forced me to share where I'd been eating beyond the places I wrote about in our Wednesday food section. I approach social media from a journalistic perspective, and over the past decade-plus, I've watched how it has transformed both what we eat and how we eat it. Now, I fully give in to supermodel pastas, Strawberry Overnight Oats (page 2), and ridiculous garnishes, and here's why you should, too.

WHO YOU ARE

The Phone Eats First Cookbook isn't necessarily for influencers with hundreds of thousands of followers—although they might get some ideas, too. It's for the everyday Instagrammer and/or TikToker who loves food and cooking and likes to share what they're eating. Heck, you don't even need to be on Instagram or TikTok to enjoy this book. It's really for anyone who cooks and wants tasty new ideas. Bonus points for a sense of humor!

It's for twenty- and thirty-somethings trying to grow their numbers, sure, but it's even more for people of all ages who are tapped into food trends on social media and

want to get creative in the kitchen and eat great food. It's for the social media–obsessed, the TikTok-agnostic, and even the Instagram skeptical, as I once was.

TikTok's creative remixes have been especially friendly to home cooking, where hacks like turning lasagna into soup, swapping pesto for butter when cooking eggs, and using rice paper sheets to wrap dumplings have changed the way we cook. And while TikTok originally skewed very young, today more than half of its users are over thirty, with those ten-second recipe videos being a major driver for, let's just say, users of a certain age.

This cookbook is for all of us everyday social media users, because we, too, can be "content creators." (Blogger hat not included.)

GET COOKING . . . AND POSTING

You're going to want to make and eat these fifty recipes ASAP, but please remember the cardinal rule of social media: The phone eats first. Before you rip apart your Accordion Potatoes (page 46) or tear into one of those S'mores Cookies (page 110), snap a photo. Then feel free to indulge in all the deliciousness and freak out over how you were today years old when you discovered the glory that is Dalgona Coffee Chocolate Cake (page 101). (Just don't forget to post on your socials with #thephoneeatsfirstcookbook.)

THE PHONE EATS FIRST COOKBOOK

BREAKFAST

One wouldn't think that oats—perhaps the most banal, the most wholesome, the most boring food—would get so much hype, but here we are, living in an era when a jar of overnight oats racks up literally billions of TikTok views. The appeal can't be explained away by convenience; there are loads of breakfasts ready in minutes, including, you know, regular oats. No, making overnight oats capitalizes on our crunchy obsession with self-care, and lets us show those people we met once on vacation three years ago that not only are we downing adorned oatmeal on the reg, but that we make it beautiful and top it with fresh fruit and granola—all before 7 a.m. Or it could just taste good. @lovelydelites's iteration is so good because instead of using run-of-the-mill flavorless milk, you start with a homemade strawberry milk.

HASHTAG PAIRING:
#overnightoathype
#mealprep #totesoats
#lookatmyoatsbeckywiththe
goodhair

PHOTO TIP: Set up by a window during the day for natural light. That's going to give you the most vibrant, bright photos to light up your feed. Bonus: Natural light is free!

SERVES 1

STRAWBERRY OVERNIGHT OATS

Hannah Kling | **@lovelydelites (lovelydelites.com)**

½ cup milk of choice

½ cup fresh strawberries, plus more for topping

½ cup old-fashioned oats

¼ cup plain yogurt of choice, plus more for topping

1½ teaspoons maple syrup

½ teaspoon vanilla extract

Granola, for topping

1. In a blender, combine the milk and ½ cup strawberries. Blend until there aren't any strawberry chunks left and the mixture is smooth and creamy, 30 to 60 seconds.

2. Transfer this strawberry milk to a large mason jar with a lid and add the oats, yogurt, maple syrup, and vanilla extract. Mix well with a spoon until all ingredients are incorporated.

3. Cover with the lid and store in the fridge for a minimum of 4 hours or up to overnight.

4. Mix the oats in the morning and top with more strawberries and granola, or whatever else you like on your oats.

For drama, you cannot beat these towering soufflé pancakes—or @pollypocketsy's TikTok account. With her theatrical, tragicomic voice, @pollypocketsy regales us with cliffhanger stories of her boyfriend, her ex-boyfriend, and her roommates, all while whipping up delicious fare like these jiggly Japanese pancakes.

Before you start, know that these take longer than regular pancakes. You have to whip those egg whites into a glossy meringue, gently whisk in the yolk batter, and then slowly layer and cook the dollops of batter. But if you put in the time, you'll get a short stack that commands Internet attention.

HASHTAG PAIRING:
#fluffypancakes #thicc #breakfastjiggle #whathappensnext???

MAKES 2 PANCAKES; SERVES 1

JAPANESE SOUFFLÉ PANCAKES

@pollypocketsy

2 large eggs

2 tablespoons whole milk

½ teaspoon vanilla extract

3 tablespoons all-purpose flour

½ teaspoon baking powder

2 tablespoons sugar

½ teaspoon freshly squeezed lemon juice

1 tablespoon neutral oil

Butter, berries, and maple syrup, for topping

1. Separate the eggs, placing the yolks in a medium bowl and the whites in a large bowl.

2. Add the milk and vanilla to the yolks. Sift the flour and baking powder into the bowl with the yolks, then whisk together.

3. Combine the sugar and lemon juice with the egg whites, then beat on medium-high with a handheld electric mixer until stiff peaks form, 5 to 7 minutes.

4. Add a large spoonful of the egg white mixture to the yolk batter and gently stir together with a large whisk. Then pour the yolk mixture into the egg white bowl and gently whisk until just combined (you don't want to deflate your egg whites).

5. Brush a skillet with the oil and set over medium-low heat. Allow to heat up for a minute or so, and then ladle two dollops (about ⅓ cup each) of the mixture onto the skillet. Add 1 tablespoon water to the skillet and cook for 3 minutes, until the batter is just starting to set. Put the remaining batter on top of each of the pancakes. Add 1 additional tablespoon of water to the skillet and cook for 4 minutes. The pancakes should be just set enough to flip. Flip and cook on the other side until the pancakes are just set and they spring back when you gently poke them, about 7 additional minutes.

6. Crown the pancakes with whatever glorious toppings you'd like, but you can't go wrong with butter, berries, and syrup.

Did you know that an egg was featured on *TIME* magazine's list of the 25 Most Influential People on the Internet? Because it was, and besides not really being a person, that's illustrative of just how much the Internet loves a good egg. It's no wonder that shakshuka recipes have racked up hundreds of millions of views. I mean, just look at it! Talk about a breakfast dish begging for its close-up. The vibrant red from the sautéed bell peppers and tomatoes, the verdant green from a generous sprinkling of parsley, and, of course, the mosaic of effortlessly beautiful poached eggs. @thechefziad's recipe comes together quickly and easily, and it is best scooped up with warm pita.

HASHTAG PAIRING:
#onepanwonder
#eggsistentialcrisis #naturalbeauty
#inarelationshipwithshakshuka

SERVES 4

SHAKSHUKA

Ziad Hariri | **@thechefziad**

2 tablespoons extra virgin olive oil

1 large white onion, diced

4 cloves garlic, minced

2 red bell peppers, seeded and diced

½ teaspoon smoked paprika, or to taste

½ teaspoon ground cumin, or to taste

Kosher salt and freshly ground black pepper, to taste

1 (28-ounce) can diced tomatoes

4 large eggs

Crumbled feta and chopped flat-leaf parsley, for topping

Warmed pita, for serving

1. Pour the olive oil into a large skillet over medium heat. Add the onion and garlic and cook, stirring occasionally, until soft and translucent, 5 to 6 minutes.

2. Add the bell peppers and cook until softened, 3 to 4 minutes. Stir in the paprika, cumin, salt, and pepper and cook until fragrant, 2 minutes.

3. Stir in the tomatoes and ¼ cup water and simmer until thickened to a sauce-like consistency, about 5 minutes.

4. Crack 4 eggs into the skillet and cover with a lid. Cook until the egg whites are set and the yolks are cooked to your desired level of runniness, 5 to 8 minutes.

5. Remove from the heat and finish with feta and parsley. Serve with pita for scooping.

Some viral recipes should be left on the Interwebs. (I'm talking to you, cooking steak in a jar, doing horrible, unthinkable things to Peeps, and using tampons to soak up excess meat grease.) But the yogurt toast trend, especially when combined with milk tea powder and boba, is most definitely one that you should pluck from TikTok's abyss and lasso into the kingdom that is your home kitchen.

Start with a loaf of unsliced brioche—that way you can control how thick and chunky your slices are—and mix your custard with milk tea powder for silky sweetness. @sweetportfolio toasts her bread in an air fryer, but if you don't have one, the toaster oven works, too. Then spoon those chubby, tapioca-filled popping boba on top for FYP-worthy toast.

HASHTAG PAIRING:
#toastofthetown #nonotes
#bobastic #thiccslices
#pleaseleavethepeepsalone

MAKES 2 SLICES; SERVES 1

BOBA TEA CUSTARD TOAST

Valentina Mussi | **@sweetportfolio**

1 large egg
¼ cup full-fat plain Greek yogurt
2 tablespoons milk tea powder

2 slices brioche bread (at least 1 inch thick)
Brown sugar boba pearls, for topping

1. Preheat an air fryer to 360°F. (If you don't have an air fryer, you can use a toaster oven set at 350°F.)

2. Mix the egg, yogurt, and milk tea powder in a small bowl.

3. Gently press down in the center of each slice of bread to make an indentation and pour the custard into the indentations until it fills them and comes up the sides to coat the remainder of the bread surfaces. Cook in the air fryer until golden brown and set, about 6 minutes. (Or place on a toaster-oven pan and toast until the bread is starting to brown and the custard is just set.)

4. Heat the boba according to the instructions on the package. Place a few spoonfuls on the toast and enjoy!

Older millennials, and people from previous generations, probably remember chia seeds as one thing: Chia Pets. (Ch-ch-ch-chia! Look it up, Gen Z.) It wasn't until the early 2010s, when Instagram made sharing pics of our virtuous breakfasts so much easier, that we upped our ingestion of the seeds and cut back on growing little chia hedgehogs out of terra-cotta statues.

Of course, chia seeds existed long before camera phones and even before Chia Pets! They were an Aztec superfood, but for some reason the Aztecs didn't take pictures of their chia smoothies and cereals, so most of us didn't realize we could consume them until much later. A tasty way to eat chia seeds is in this dessert-for-breakfast pumpkin pie pudding. (It might be a little borderline on the virtuousness, but since chia seeds are loaded with antioxidants, fiber, omega-3s, and vitamin B, we're going with it.) More than a decade after starting to make the social media rounds, chia seeds are still trending, with chia-related recipes on TikTok racking up a couple hundred million views and counting.

HASHTAG PAIRING:
#chchchchia #pumpkinspicelover
#dessertbreakfast
#youcaneatthehedgehog

SERVES 1

PUMPKIN PIE CHIA PUDDING

Kristi Roeder | **@avocado_skillet (avocadoskillet.com)**

3 tablespoons chia seeds

3 tablespoons pumpkin puree

1 tablespoon maple syrup

½ teaspoon pumpkin pie spice

¼ teaspoon vanilla extract

¾ cup milk of choice

Whipped cream, pecans, ground cinnamon, and cinnamon sticks for topping

1. Mix the chia seeds, pumpkin puree, syrup, pumpkin pie spice, vanilla extract, and milk in a serving glass or a mason jar until fully combined. Cover and refrigerate. After 10 minutes, stir to prevent clumping. Refrigerate until the chia seeds absorb the liquid and take on a gel-like texture, at least 1 hour or up to overnight.

2. Top with whipped cream, pecans, and ground cinnamon. Add a cinnamon stick, and relish the fact that you're eating pudding for breakfast.

PESTO EGG AVOCADO TOAST

Bailey Rhatigan | **@sailor_bailey (sailorbailey.com)**

like gun violence and our broken ice maker, the prevalence of oddly topped toasts in our feed is a problem we just refuse to solve, so at least for the toasts, you might as well give in and figure out how to artfully cover bread. Of course, the Beyoncé of all toasted bread is avocado toast, and @sailor_bailey brings it into the 2020s by combining it with another huge social media trend: pesto eggs.

Her spin on pesto is a bright, nutty blend of walnuts, spinach, and Parmesan. This delicious and vibrant toast will light up your photos, your life, and maybe even the world. (Well, not the world, sadly; see: gun violence.)

HASHTAG PAIRING:
#toastwiththemostest
#pestoeggs #dailybread
#wantocado?havocado!
#seriouslymoretoast?

MAKES 2 SLICES; SERVES 1

3 cups fresh spinach

⅓ cup walnut halves

¼ cup chopped cilantro leaves and stems

¼ cup grated or shaved Parmesan

2 cloves garlic

⅓ cup extra virgin olive oil, plus more as needed

Juice of 1 large lemon (about 3 tablespoons)

¼ teaspoon red pepper flakes, plus more for garnish

¼ teaspoon kosher salt

2 large eggs

2 slices bakery-style bread

1 large ripe avocado, pitted, peeled, and sliced

1. Put the spinach, walnuts, cilantro, Parmesan, garlic, ⅓ cup olive oil, lemon juice, ¼ teaspoon red pepper flakes, and salt in a food processor fitted with the metal blade or a blender and blitz until it forms a loose paste. If the paste is too thick, thin with additional olive oil.

2. Spread 2 tablespoons of the pesto in a medium nonstick skillet and place over medium heat. Heat until the pesto is starting to bubble, 1 to 2 minutes, then crack the eggs onto the pesto. Cook for 1 to 2 minutes, then cover with a lid and cook until the whites are set and yolks have reached the desired stage of runniness, 1 to 2 additional minutes.

3. Meanwhile, lightly toast the bread, then spread each slice with 1 tablespoon pesto. Top each piece of toast with half of the avocado, a fried egg, and more pesto. Garnish with red pepper flakes.

Remember way back in 2020, when we were so scared to touch anything that we wore gloves and carried antibacterial wipes with us everywhere? And then a year later, when we slathered room temperature butter directly onto bacteria-laden cutting boards and double-dipped into it with dozens of strangers? Our butter era sparked hundreds of millions of views, a butter shortage, and, presumably, a spike in cardiologist visits.

Of all the spinoff boards (nut butters! frosting! Vegemite!), my favorite is @smittenkitchen's cream cheese board. She tops a mountain of cream cheese with chives, dill, capers, and everything bagel seasoning and accessorizes with sliced cucumbers, red onion, and tomato. Don't forget a depraved amount of lox and bagels (whether you toast or not is between you and your God) and you have a brunch board that could not be easier or more impressive.

HASHTAG PAIRINGS:
#inourcreamcheeseera
#babyneedscalcium
#cantstopwontstop
#saturatedfatwho?

SERVES 8 TO 12

BAGEL AND CREAM CHEESE BOARD

Deb Perelman | **@smittenkitchen (smittenkitchen.com)**

2 (8-ounce) packages cream cheese, softened

1 cucumber, peeled and sliced

1 to 2 large ripe tomatoes, thinly sliced

1 small red onion, sliced into rings

½ lemon, sliced

½ cup capers

1 pound sliced lox

8 to 12 bagels

Snipped chives, everything bagel seasoning, uncut chives, and dill sprigs for garnish

1. Plop the softened cream cheese onto a cutting board or serving tray. Swirl the cream cheese with a butter knife or spreader (this will create little pools to prevent toppings from sliding off).

2. Arrange the cucumber, tomato, red onion, lemon slices, capers, and lox around the cream cheese.

3. Slice the bagels and toast them, if desired.

4. Sprinkle the cream cheese with snipped chives and everything bagel seasoning. Garnish the platter with chives and dill. Dip in and enjoy!

MILLENNIAL PINK SMOOTHIE BOWL

Allyson Reedy | **@allysoneatsden**

t's a smoothie, but in a bowl! The superfood (or just super pretty, depending on how much you buy into health and wellness trends) that kickstarted the smoothie bowl craze was the acai berry, which needed to be frozen in order to be shipped, thus making it a highly scoopable bowl food once we got our hot little hands (and blenders) on it. And once we saw those gorgeous purple bowls on our feeds, we decided, for really no good reason, to put more pureed fruits into bowls. So thank you social media for keeping us free from scurvy. (Phew!)

Around that same time in the 2010s, we were making absolutely everything in pink, so we then decided—again, for really no good reason—to make our smoothie bowls millennial pink, too. Perfect for the generation raised on donut-flavored Dunkin' cereal, the millennial pink smoothie bowl tapped into our concentric desires to eat better and to post colorful foods on Insta. My simple blend of berries, banana, and vanilla yogurt in this bowl gets all dolled up with pretty much whatever beautiful, edible small things I have on hand, like coconut flakes, fresh mint leaves, and pomegranate seeds. (But don't worry if you're not the type of person who has coconut flakes, fresh mint leaves, and pomegranate seeds on hand in the morning. Throw on whatever toppings you like.)

¾ cup vanilla yogurt

¾ cup milk of choice

¾ cup frozen raspberries

¾ cup frozen strawberries

½ frozen banana

1 tablespoon coconut flakes

Fresh raspberries, banana slices, mint leaves, and pomegranate seeds for garnish

1. Combine the yogurt, milk, and frozen raspberries, strawberries, and banana in a blender and puree until smooth.

2. Transfer the mixture to a bowl and, as skillfully as you can muster early in the morning, garnish with the coconut flakes, fresh raspberries, banana slices, mint leaves, and pomegranate seeds. Post on social for all to see.

HASHTAG PAIRING:
#smoothiebowl #plantbased
#eatdrinkandbeberry #okboomer

PHOTO TIP: When in doubt, overhead it out. Try to get as close to 90 degrees with your phone as possible, hold still, and shoot!

SERVES 1

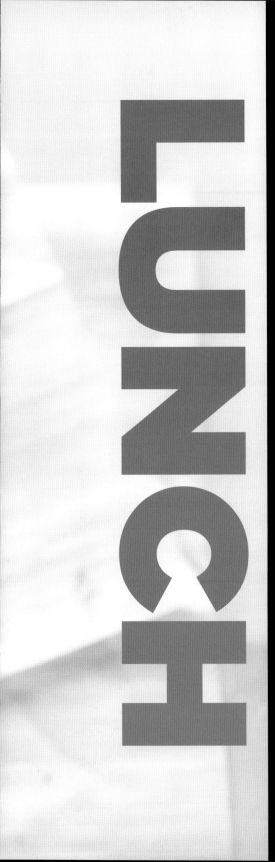

LUNCH

CRUNCH WRAPS
Lehandra Staude, @lehandrabreanne

GREEK CHICKEN WRAPS
Christina Meehan, @flavorsbyfrangipane
(flavorsbyfrangipane.com)

NASHVILLE HOT CHICKEN
Gideon General, @gidsgids

ICE CUBE TRAY SUSHI
Michelle Tiang, @michelletiang on
TikTok, @mitz_tiang on IG

DONUT GRILLED CHEESE
WITH TOMATO SOUP
Darryl Harmon, @clintonhallny

TERIYAKI SALMON SALAD WITH
CRISPY RICE CROUTONS
Darlene Schrijver, @thesaladlab on TikTok,
@thesaladlabofficial on IG

RICE PAPER DUMPLINGS
Jess Pryles, @jesspryles (jesspryles.com)

LASAGNA SOUP
Snejana Andreeva, @themodernnonna
(themodernnonna.com)

CHOPPED TURKEY SANDWICHES
Boyd Brown III, @chef_boydbrownthe3rd on TikTok,
@boydbrown3 on IG (chefboydbrowniii.com)

CRUNCH WRAPS

Lehandra Staude | @lehandrabreanne

n summer 2005—before we bailed out Wall Street banks, but after we gave billions to the airlines (the first time)—Taco Bell introduced the Crunchwrap Supreme as a temporary menu item. But it's not like they could take away the nectar of the gods once we'd tasted it, and by 2006, the Crunchwrap had earned its status as a full-fledged, permanent T-Bell menu item.

Fifteen years later—right around when we bailed out the airlines for the second time—the Internet took it upon itself to improve the crispy hexagon that dreams are made of. @lehandrabreanne says the key is slathering the hot ingredients—like the nacho cheese sauce and taco meat—on the bottom layers, then separating the cold lettuce, tomato, cabbage, and sour cream with a crunchy tostada shell. The result is a handheld meal good enough to make us forget that our tax dollars went to millionaires and billionaires while we're relegated to $4.99 fast-food fare.

HASHTAG PAIRING: #crunchwrap #easyrecipe #tbellvibes #sillybankers

PHOTO TIP: Stack your wraps for maximum effect, using toothpicks to keep your T-Bell tower stable.

SERVES 4

1 pound lean ground beef

1 (1¼-ounce) packet taco seasoning

5 (9- to 10-inch) tortillas

1 cup nacho cheese sauce

4 tostada shells

¼ to ½ cup sour cream

1 medium ripe tomato, chopped

1 small head iceberg lettuce, shredded

1 small head purple cabbage, shredded

1. Brown the ground beef in a large skillet over medium-high heat. Add the taco seasoning and follow the directions on the packet to finish cooking.

2. Put a tortilla on a work surface. Spread ¼ cup of nacho cheese in the center of the tortilla, leaving a 2-inch margin free around the perimeter. Arrange ¼ of the meat mixture on top of the cheese sauce. Place a tostada shell on top of the meat. Spread 1 to 2 tablespoons sour cream on the tostada shell. Scatter on tomato, lettuce, and cabbage. Repeat with 3 more of the tortillas.

3. Cut the remaining tortilla into quarters. Place a tortilla quarter on top of one of the unfolded crunch wraps. Fold the edges of the wrap around the tortilla wedge, so that the filling is completely covered and the package resembles a hexagon. Repeat with the remaining tortilla wedges and wraps.

4. Heat a skillet or griddle over medium heat. Place one wrap folded side down in the skillet. Cook until just starting to brown and crisp, about 30 seconds, then flip and cook until browned on the other side, about 30 additional seconds. Repeat with the remaining wraps. Halve each and serve piping hot.

Social media is thirsty for dogs wearing clothes, woman-yelling-at-cat memes, and good chicken recipes. Bonus points for whoever can combine all three, but for now we'll stick to this Greek chicken wrap from @flavorsbyfrangipane, who challenged her followers to tell her the recipe they could eat every single day and never get sick of. Hers is this viral chicken wrap, and while the recipe is a little long for our TLDR culture, it's way easier than it looks.

@flavorsbyfrangipane makes her own garlic naan, but it's totally fine for us mortals to buy it premade at the store. Another concession: grilling the chicken gives it a nice smoky flavor, but you can also throw it in a skillet if the weather's cold/you don't own a grill/putting on shoes just sounds too hard. It's still going to be obsession-worthy.

HASHTAG PAIRING:
#chickensofinstagram
#tldr #obsessionfoods
#whywontmydogwearhats?

SERVES 4

GREEK CHICKEN WRAPS

Christina Meehan | **@flavorsbyfrangipane (flavorsbyfrangipane.com)**

CHICKEN

4 boneless, skinless chicken breasts or thighs

1 cup full-fat plain Greek yogurt

1 tablespoon extra virgin olive oil

1 tablespoon Dijon mustard

1 teaspoon dried oregano

1 teaspoon dried thyme

1 teaspoon kosher salt

1 teaspoon freshly ground black pepper

Juice of 2 medium lemons (about ¼ cup)

TZATZIKI

1 medium cucumber

1½ cups full-fat plain Greek yogurt

2 cloves garlic, minced

2 tablespoons chopped dill or 1 teaspoon dried dill, plus more as needed

Juice of 1 medium lemon (about 2 tablespoons), plus more as needed

1 tablespoon extra virgin olive oil

½ teaspoon kosher salt, plus more as needed

¼ teaspoon freshly ground black pepper, plus more as needed

SALAD AND SERVING

4 medium tomatoes, diced

2 medium cucumbers, seeded and diced

1 small red onion, thinly sliced

2 tablespoons extra virgin olive oil

Juice of 1 medium lemon (about 2 tablespoons)

Kosher salt and freshly ground black pepper, to taste

4 pieces garlic naan, warmed

1. **MAKE THE CHICKEN:** In a large bowl, combine the chicken with the yogurt, olive oil, mustard, oregano, thyme, salt, pepper, and lemon juice. Cover the bowl with plastic wrap and allow the mixture to marinate in the refrigerator for at least 1 hour or up to 12 hours for maximum flavor.

2. **MAKE THE TZATZIKI:** Peel the cucumber, cut it in half lengthwise, and use a spoon to scrape out the seeds. Grate the cucumber using a box grater or a food processor. Place the grated cucumber in a clean kitchen towel or cheesecloth and squeeze out as much moisture as possible. This will help prevent the tzatziki from becoming too watery.

3. In a medium bowl, combine the grated cucumber, yogurt, garlic, dill, lemon juice, olive oil, salt, and pepper. Stir until well combined. Taste and adjust dill, lemon juice, salt, and pepper as needed. Cover with plastic wrap and refrigerate for at least 30 minutes and up to 12 hours to allow the flavors to meld.

4. Back to the chicken! For optimal taste, grill the chicken. Alternatively, you can use the stovetop. For grilling, preheat your grill to 375°F. Place the chicken on the preheated grill, close the lid, and cook 6 to 8 minutes. Flip the chicken and cook 5 to 7 minutes, until the internal temperature reaches 165°F. On the stovetop, heat a large skillet over medium heat for 2 to 3 minutes. Place chicken in the skillet and cook without disturbing until browned, 5 to 7 minutes. Flip the chicken and cook 5 to 7 additional minutes, until the internal temperature reaches 165°F.

5. MAKE THE SALAD: In a large salad bowl, combine the tomatoes, cucumbers, and onion. In a separate small bowl, whisk together the olive oil and lemon juice. Drizzle the mixture over the salad and season with salt and pepper. Gently toss the salad to coat with the dressing.

6. Slice the cooked chicken into cubes or strips. Place a garlic naan on a work surface and layer one side with chicken, tzatziki, and cucumber salad. Fold the top over the filling. Repeat for the remaining servings.

How do you make fried chicken pop on social? Make it red! And shiny! Besides achieving the very important goal of making plain old brown chicken look pretty, hot chicken > regular fried chicken in terms of flavor. (Hey, those Nashvillians were onto something!) @gidsgids's chicken tenders just might be the world's crunchiest thanks to the refrigerated batter and double fry, maximizing your ASMR audio. Feel free to play around with the amount of cayenne pepper, depending on your spice tolerance and/or just how ungodly red you want your chicken photo to be.

HASHTAG PAIRING:
#fireemoji #frymeariver #paintitred #nashvilleisonit #asmrismylovelanguage

SERVES 4 TO 5

NASHVILLE HOT CHICKEN

Gideon General | **@gidsgids**

CHICKEN AND RUB

3 tablespoons kosher salt

2 tablespoons garlic powder

1 tablespoon onion powder

1 tablespoon freshly ground black pepper

1 teaspoon MSG (optional)

10 to 15 chicken tenderloins

BATTER

1 large egg

⅓ cup all-purpose flour

½ cup cold water

SEASONED FLOUR

2 cups all-purpose flour

3 tablespoons chicken soup powder, preferably Osem or Knorr

1 tablespoon garlic powder

1 tablespoon onion powder

1½ teaspoons smoked paprika

1½ teaspoons freshly ground black pepper

1 teaspoon Chinese five spice powder (optional)

1 teaspoon white pepper

1 teaspoon dry mustard

¼ teaspoon kosher salt

FRYING

1 quart canola oil or vegetable oil

1 to 2 cups all-purpose flour

HOT CHICKEN OIL AND SERVING

1 cup hot frying oil

2 to 3 tablespoons ground cayenne

1 to 2 tablespoons smoked paprika

1 tablespoon brown sugar

1 teaspoon freshly ground black pepper

1 teaspoon garlic powder

½ teaspoon kosher salt

Pickles, for serving (optional)

1. **MAKE THE RUB:** Mix the salt, garlic and onion powders, black pepper, and MSG, if using, in a small bowl. Place the chicken in a large baking dish and season the chicken pieces all over with the rub. Loosely cover the chicken with plastic wrap and refrigerate for at least 1 hour and up to 8 hours.

2. **MAKE THE BATTER:** As soon as you have prepared the chicken, combine the egg, flour, and cold water in a medium bowl.

(continued)

Refrigerate until needed, for at least 1 hour or up to 8 hours. Making the batter ahead of time is the key to achieving maximum crunch.

3. **MAKE THE SEASONED FLOUR:** In a large bowl, whisk together all the ingredients. Set aside.

4. **FRY THE CHICKEN:** Place the oil in a large pot with high sides and bring to 300°F. Set a wire rack on a baking sheet.

5. Place the flour for frying on a large plate. Arrange the batter and the seasoned flour next to it. Using your hands, lightly coat a piece of chicken in the plain flour. Then, dip in the batter to coat completely. Shake off any excess batter and dredge in the seasoned flour. Press firmly to make sure the chicken is coated. Set on a clean plate and repeat with the remaining pieces.

6. Carefully add the chicken to the hot oil, working in batches to avoid crowding the pan. Fry the chicken for 5 minutes, then use tongs to transfer to the wire rack.

7. Once all the chicken is fried, increase the temperature of the oil to 350°F and fry in batches for a second time until golden brown and crispy, 2 to 3 minutes. Transfer to the wire rack.

8. **MAKE THE HOT CHICKEN OIL:** Use a heatproof cup measure to scoop out 1 cup of the frying oil. Pour this into a large heatproof bowl. Add the cayenne, paprika, brown sugar, black pepper, garlic powder, and salt and mix to incorporate.

9. While the fried chicken and the oil are still hot, dip the chicken in the seasoned oil and return to the wire rack. Plate 2 or 3 pieces per serving and enjoy with pickles, if desired.

Craving sushi but don't want to put in the effort of forming or rolling it? Stick it in an ice cube tray! Making sushi in an ice cube tray has to go on the imaginary list of top-ten best social media hacks. It's the clever party trick you never knew you needed. And while you probably don't actually need it, per se, don't you really, really want it?

@michelletiang makes two types of sushi, a shrimp version and another with tuna and avocado, but feel free to put your own spin on it and use salmon, krab, or whatever you can fish out of the nearest creek. (Kidding—do not eat what you get out of your creek!) In addition to the serving suggestions, you can top the sushi with eel sauce and tobiko (those little orange fish eggs you get at sushi restaurants).

HASHTAG PAIRING: #diysushi #icetrayqueen #shrimplythebest #aintnopartylikeanicecube-traysushiparty

PHOTO TIP: For more contrast and deeper shadows, shoot near a large window in midday sun.

MAKES 24 PIECES; SERVES 2 TO 3

ICE CUBE TRAY SUSHI

Michelle Tiang | **@michelletiang on TikTok** | **@mitz_tiang on IG**

⅓ cup sushi rice

1 tablespoon unseasoned rice vinegar

12 cooked cocktail shrimp

12 slices sushi-grade tuna, cut to fit ice cube tray indentations

1 avocado, pitted, peeled, and thinly sliced into 24 pieces

Wasabi and Kewpie mayonnaise, for topping

Pickled ginger, wasabi, and soy sauce, for serving

1. Combine the sushi rice and ½ cup water in a medium saucepan. Soak the rice off the heat for 15 minutes. Then bring to a boil over high heat. Reduce the heat to low, cover, and simmer until the water is absorbed, 5 to 10 minutes. Remove the pot from the heat and let it sit, covered, for 10 minutes.

2. Fluff the rice with a fork and transfer to a bowl. Mix in the vinegar and set aside.

3. Place a shrimp curved side up on a work surface. With a sharp knife, slice down the center of the shrimp lengthwise without going all the way through so the halves remain attached. Gently flatten the shrimp. Repeat with the remaining shrimp.

4. Line two 12-indentation ice cube trays with plastic wrap, pressing the wrap into the indentations. Place each shrimp into the 12 indentations. Place each piece of tuna into the remaining 12 indentations.

5. Top each with a slice of avocado. Divide the rice among the indentations. Press down to pack firmly and make the top even. Refrigerate for 30 minutes.

(continued)

6. Flip the ice cube trays onto a flat surface and carefully remove the sushi. Top each piece of tuna with a dab of wasabi. Top each piece of shrimp with a dab of mayo. Serve with pickled ginger, wasabi, and soy sauce for dipping.

Can multiple horsemen of the apocalypse arrive at the same time? If so, they are present here in this dish, which single-handedly brought social-media fame to the Clinton Hall restaurants across New York City. Dreamed up by owner Aristotle Hatzigeorgiou and executed by chef Darryl Harmon, it has a ridiculous cheese pull, a killer dunk, and something on a doughnut that should never be on a doughnut. And yet it works. The sharpness of the tomato soup cuts the richness of the grilled cheese doughnut, and it all comes together in one harmonious, apocalypse-inducing bite.

HASHTAG PAIRING: #saycheese #soupseason #glazedandconfused #apocalypsefood

SERVES 2

DONUT GRILLED CHEESE WITH TOMATO SOUP

Darryl Harmon | **@clintonhallny**

SOUP

1 teaspoon extra virgin olive oil

¼ cup chopped Spanish onion

1 teaspoon chopped garlic

1 (14.5-ounce) can whole peeled plum tomatoes in juice

1 teaspoon chopped basil leaves

½ teaspoon sugar

¼ teaspoon dried oregano

Kosher salt and freshly ground black pepper, to taste

1 tablespoon unsalted butter

GRILLED CHEESE

1 tablespoon unsalted butter

2 glazed doughnuts

6 ounces mozzarella, shredded

1. MAKE THE TOMATO SOUP: Heat the oil in a large pot over medium heat. Sauté the onion and garlic until softened, about 5 minutes.

2. Add the tomatoes and cook for 20 minutes. Stir in the basil, sugar, and oregano and season to taste with salt and pepper.

3. Remove the pot from the heat and stir in the butter. Puree until smooth with an immersion blender (or remove solids to a traditional blender, puree, and stir back into the liquid). Taste and adjust seasoning. Keep the soup warm over low heat while you make the grilled cheese.

4. MAKE THE GRILLED CHEESE: Heat a griddle to medium heat (300°F, if you have one with a temperature gauge) and melt the butter on it. Halve the doughnuts lengthwise and place them on the griddle, cut (unglazed) sides down.

5. Evenly distribute the mozzarella on the 4 glazed sides of the doughnuts. Cover the griddle with a stainless steel cover (or a large pot lid or tented foil) to melt the cheese evenly.

(continued)

6. Once the cheese has melted, press the two halves of each doughnut together with the grilled sides on the outside. Divide the soup between two serving bowls, and, if you want to create an authentic Clinton Hall experience, hang each sandwich on a banana hook over the tomato soup. Otherwise, serve on a plate alongside the soup. Dip the sandwich into the soup for ultimate deliciousness.

The Internet loves a good salad. (See viral green goddess salad, hot-girl summer salad, and the Jennifer Aniston salad that she supposedly ate for ten years straight on the set of *Friends*, though it turned out to not be that salad after all.) The queen of creative, craveable, and—perhaps most importantly for the purposes of our egos—viral salads is @thesaladlab, and this bowl illustrates why. The teriyaki salmon gives it deliciously sweet/umami-rific heft, the crispy rice croutons take it totally over the top, you'll want to eat the spicy, creamy dressing by the spoonful, and the colors all come together for a beautiful shot. Oh, and as for that Jennifer Aniston salad? Rachel Green herself weighed in on the Lab's take, calling it "incredible." So yes, @thesaladlab, your work here is done.

HASHTAG PAIRING:
#saladsoftiktok #teriyakitime #srirachamakeseverythingbetter #rossandrachel4ever

SERVES 4

TERIYAKI SALMON SALAD WITH CRISPY RICE CROUTONS

Darlene Schrijver | @thesaladlab on TikTok | @thesaladlabofficial on IG (thesaladlab.net)

4 cups cooked sushi rice

¼ cup mirin

1 tablespoon olive oil or avocado oil cooking spray

1 pound skinless salmon, cut into 1½-inch cubes

2 tablespoons teriyaki sauce

½ cup Kewpie mayonnaise

½ cup sriracha

2 tablespoons honey

2 tablespoons toasted sesame seeds

2 teaspoons sesame oil

4 cups shredded Napa or Savoy cabbage (½ small head)

4 cups hand-torn butter lettuce (½ small head)

1 large English cucumber, diced

1 large avocado, pitted, peeled, and diced

1 red bell pepper, cut into 1-inch matchsticks

4 scallions, chopped

4 watermelon or daikon radishes, cut into ¼-inch dice

1 jalapeño, seeded, sliced, and sauteed

2 tablespoons furikake

1. In a large bowl, mix the rice and mirin to combine. Transfer to a parchment-lined baking sheet and flatten to an even ¾- to 1-inch thickness. Place another sheet of parchment paper and another baking sheet on top, press down, and freeze for at least 1 hour.

2. Preheat the oven to 425°F. Remove the rice from the freezer and cut into 1-inch cubes. Arrange the cubes of rice in a single layer on a parchment-lined baking sheet and spray with oil. Bake until the edges start to brown, 25 to 30 minutes. Keep the oven on.

3. In a medium bowl, toss the salmon cubes in the teriyaki sauce to coat. Cover and refrigerate for 20 minutes. Transfer the salmon to a parchment-lined baking sheet and bake to your desired doneness, 7 to 10 minutes.

4. In a large salad bowl, whisk together the mayonnaise, sriracha, honey, sesame seeds, and sesame oil.

5. Add the cabbage, lettuce, cucumber, avocado, bell pepper, scallions, radishes, jalapeño, salmon, rice croutons, and furikake. Toss to combine. Divide among 4 salad plates or bowls.

Since @okonomikitchen posted her rice paper dumpling video in July 2021, millions upon millions of people have had their lives changed by these crunchy, versatile, way-easier-to-fold-than-actual-dumpling dumplings. Seriously, if you add up the views for the plethora of rice paper dumpling recipes on TikTok and Instagram, you'll get a number that rivals the GDP of a small Baltic country.

For this version by Texas barbecue expert @jesspryles, the crispy/chewy little pillows are stuffed with pork and rehydrated shiitake mushrooms for an umami-filled bite. You could easily skip the pork and swap out the fish sauce for soy to make them vegetarian. @jesspryles dips hers in nuoc cham, but I like these with a dipping sauce of equal parts soy sauce and rice vinegar fired up with chili crisp. If you're new to rolling dumplings, you might want to double-wrap these to give them a better chance of staying in one piece.

MAKES 10 DUMPLINGS; SERVES 2 TO 3

RICE PAPER DUMPLINGS

Jess Pryles | **@jesspryles (jesspryles.com)**

1 ounce dried shiitake mushrooms

1 pound ground pork

2 to 4 scallions, thinly sliced, plus more for garnish

¼ cup chopped mint leaves

¼ cup chopped cilantro leaves

2 cloves garlic, crushed

1 tablespoon minced ginger

1 tablespoon fish sauce

2 tablespoons sugar

2 teaspoons kosher salt

10 or 20 sheets rice paper

½ cup canola oil or vegetable oil

Low-sodium soy sauce, unseasoned rice vinegar, and chili crisp, for dipping

Sesame seeds, for garnish

1. Put the mushrooms in a small bowl and add boiling water to cover. Soak until flexible, 10 to 15 minutes, then drain and squeeze out any excess liquid. Remove and discard the hard stems and finely dice.

2. Combine the mushrooms with the pork, scallions, mint, cilantro, garlic, ginger, fish sauce, 1 tablespoon sugar, and salt and stir with a large spoon to fully incorporate.

3. In a separate small bowl, combine the remaining 1 tablespoon sugar with 2 cups of water and stir until dissolved.

4. Place one rice paper sheet (or two, if you're double-wrapping) on a work surface. Use a pastry or basting brush to moisten the sheet on both sides with the sugar-water mixture until it is flexible enough to fold, 30 to 60 seconds. (This is the best way to soften the sheets without making them too tacky to work with.)

5. Place 2 to 3 tablespoons of the filling in the top middle of the rice paper sheet. Fold the top over the filling, then fold in each

side. Now, finish rolling up the little pillow-shaped dumpling. (But really you can fold them any way you like!) Set the dumpling aside on parchment paper and repeat until you have used up all the rice papers and filling. If not using immediately, cover and refrigerate for up to 3 hours.

6. Heat a large nonstick skillet over medium-high heat and add the oil. Give the oil 2 minutes to heat up, then add several dumplings, being sure there is space between them. Work in batches to avoid crowding the pan—the dumplings will stick together if they're touching. Cook until the bottoms are just starting to brown and crisp, 5 to 7 minutes, then turn and cook until browned on all sides. With a slotted spoon, remove to a large plate lined with paper towels to drain. Allow the dumplings to cool slightly. Make a dipping sauce of equal parts soy sauce and rice vinegar with a heaping spoonful of chili crisp. Transfer the dumplings to a serving platter, garnish with sliced scallions and sesame seeds, and enjoy!

When a recipe video racks up views into the hundreds of millions, it typically means one of two things: it's either really, really strange (turning pasta into chips, anyone?) or it's really, really tasty. Lasagna soup is the latter, and @themodernnonna's take nails the cheesy, tomato-y, garlicky dish we love, only in a way-easier-to-make soup form. Our beloved nonna says you can use pretty much whatever ground meat you like, but I use Italian sausage to give it an extra kick.

HASHTAG PAIRING: #makeitsoup #hastalasagna #soupweather #getthatricotta

SERVES 4

LASAGNA SOUP

Snejana Andreeva | **@themodernnonna (themodernnonna.com)**

3 tablespoons extra virgin olive oil

1 pound ground pork, turkey, beef, or sausage

1 medium yellow onion, finely chopped

4 cloves garlic, minced

1 rib celery, minced (optional)

2¼ teaspoons Italian seasoning or dried oregano

Kosher salt and freshly ground black pepper, to taste

1 tablespoon tomato paste

1 cup tomato sauce or tomato puree

1 Parmesan rind (optional)

3½ cups water or unsalted vegetable broth

5 ounces (18 pieces) fettucce ricce pasta or lasagna noodles

½ cup full-fat ricotta

Basil leaves and grated Parmesan, for garnish

Crusty bread, for serving

1. In a large pot over medium-high heat, combine the olive oil and ground meat. Cook, using a wooden spoon to break the meat into chunks, until the liquid has fully evaporated and the meat is browned, about 10 minutes. (Keep in mind that ground turkey will not brown.)

2. Reduce the heat to medium-low. Add the onion, garlic, and celery, if using, and stir. Add the Italian seasoning, season with salt and pepper, and stir. Add the tomato paste and stir to combine. Stir in the tomato sauce. (Our nonna wants us to stir between each ingredient.) Add the Parmesan rind, if using.

3. Stir in the water and the pasta. (@themodernnonna breaks each piece of pasta into 3 pieces before adding it to the pot.) Cook over medium-low heat until the pasta is al dente, about 20 minutes, but don't be shy about taste-testing.

4. Take the pot off the heat. Remove and discard the Parmesan rind, if using. Divide the soup among 4 serving bowls. Add a generous dollop of ricotta to each. Top with basil and grated cheese, and enjoy with your favorite loaf of bread!

The concept here is simple: you chop up all the ingredients for a sandwich—the meat, cheese, and veggies—then mix them up real good and scoop them onto your bread. Voilà! You get evenly distributed fillings with each and every bite. It's such a genius idea and so easy to do, it's no wonder that the chopped sandwich went viral in 2023. @chef_boydbrownthe3rd perfected his diced turkey version after trying one at a Brooklyn sandwich shop, but there are no rules, exact measurements, or judgments associated with the chopped sandwich, so feel free to go wild with the pepperoncini.

HASHTAG PAIRING:
#coldturkey #chopchop
#dontforgetthepepperoncinis
#howdidnoonethinkofthissooner?

SERVES 2

CHOPPED TURKEY SANDWICHES

Boyd Brown III | **@chef_boydbrownthe3rd on TikTok** | **@boydbrown3 on IG (chefboydbrowniii.com)**

4 thin slices tomato

½ small onion, thinly sliced

4 pepperoncini

1 cup chopped iceberg lettuce

4 slices Swiss cheese

6 slices turkey, preferably organic

2 to 3 tablespoons mayonnaise

2 large, soft hoagie rolls or similar sandwich rolls

Chips, for serving

1. Place a couple of large pieces of parchment paper on a cutting board. Arrange the tomato, onion, pepperoncini, lettuce, cheese, and turkey on the parchment paper. Chop the ingredients until they are combined thoroughly and at your desired level of chunkiness.

2. Using the paper, transfer the chopped ingredients to a medium bowl and add the mayonnaise. Mix everything with a large spoon.

3. Halve the rolls and divide the chopped mixture among the bottom halves. Top with the remaining halves and serve with your favorite chips.

SNACKS & SIDES

Yes, there are plenty of dumb stunt and idiotic challenge videos on TikTok, but there are also the brilliant, can't-believe-we-hadn't-thought-of-that cooking hack videos that revolutionize the way we eat. This is just such a recipe, where a simple potato is carved into a beautifully furrowed vessel to host everything from cheese to garlic butter and bacon in its tater-y crevices.

While they may not be a purely TikTok invention—the Swedish get credit for that via their ingenious Hasselback potatoes—we can thank social media for letting most of us know that these beauties exist. And really, why hadn't we non-Swedes thought of slicing our potatoes in a way that allows all the best stuff to melt into every bite?

HASHTAG PAIRING:
#potatopov #playwithyourfood #squeezeboxspuds #crevicelife

VIDEO TIP: It's all about the cut, so practice with a tater or two before snapping your perfect accordion. Once you've got it, make a video pushing and pulling these little guys to best show their squishiness.

SERVES 4

ACCORDION POTATOES

Calvin Kang | **@cooklikeimbook (cooklikeimbook.com)**

4 medium russet potatoes

8 ounces cheddar cheese, thinly sliced

4 tablespoons (½ stick) unsalted butter, melted

4 cloves garlic, minced

2 tablespoons grated Parmesan

1 tablespoon minced flat-leaf parsley

Kosher salt and freshly ground black pepper, to taste

¼ cup minced chives

1. Preheat the oven to 425°F. Line a baking sheet with parchment paper or aluminum foil.

2. Place two chopsticks along each long side of a potato, so that when you make a cut with your knife, it hits the chopsticks and does not go all the way through the potato. Make thin cuts all the way down the potato, so that it looks like an accordion. Repeat with the remaining potatoes. Transfer to the prepared baking sheet.

3. Place thin slices of cheddar cheese in the potato cuts.

4. Bake until the cheese is melted and the potatoes are soft, 35 to 45 minutes. While the potatoes are cooking, mix the butter, garlic, Parmesan, and parsley in a small bowl. Season to taste with salt and pepper. Once the potatoes are tender, broil them until the slices are just starting to crisp up and brown along the edges, 5 minutes.

5. Brush the potatoes with the garlic butter, getting it into all those nooks and crannies. Garnish with chives and serve hot.

We're living in times when six-year-olds practice lockdown drills at school and billionaires buy 500-million-dollar yachts. Meanwhile, the rest of us are on hold with insurance companies trying to figure out why they denied our claims. The question isn't why we should make hot pink hummus, but why aren't we making hot pink everything? These are not times for the timid and the beige; these are times to amp up each and every item we eat with the vibrant, electric pink given to us by beets. Hot pink lasagna! Hot pink shakshuka! Or just start with this hot pink hummus, because come on, what else are you going to do while you're on hold trying to get your kid's flu shot covered?

HASHTAG PAIRING:
#downwithtaupe
#beetit #barbiegirldip
#hummusbutmakeitbeets
#lifeistooshortforneutrals

SERVES 4

BEET HUMMUS

Kimberly Yang | **@cookim_mama**

2 medium beets, or half 15-ounce can beets, drained

¼ cup extra virgin olive oil, plus more for drizzling

1 (15-ounce) can chickpeas, drained and skins removed

¼ cup well-stirred tahini

2 cloves garlic

Juice of 1 medium lemon (about 2 tablespoons)

1 teaspoon ground cumin

1 teaspoon kosher salt

½ teaspoon ground coriander

½ teaspoon smoked paprika

Chopped flat-leaf parsley and sesame seeds, for garnish

Baby carrots, celery sticks, and pita triangles, for serving

1. If using raw beets, cook according to the following instructions (if using canned beets, skip to Step 2). Preheat the oven to 400°F. Wash the beets, chop off the stem ends, drizzle with olive oil, and wrap up in foil, then place on a small baking sheet. Bake until the beets are tender enough that a paring knife slides in easily, about 1 hour. Allow to cool.

2. Place the beets, chickpeas, ¼ cup of the olive oil, tahini, garlic, lemon juice, cumin, salt, coriander, and paprika in a blender and puree until smooth. If the puree is very stiff, add water in small amounts.

3. Scoop the hummus into a bowl for serving. Garnish with parsley, sesame seeds, and a drizzle of olive oil. Serve with carrots, celery, and pita for dipping.

Often, it's the simplest recipes that go viral. (Grilled PB&J, anyone?) This makes sense, as most of us do not want to spend three hours searching a multitude of specialty grocers for ingredients and then another three frantically YouTubing how to properly fold our soufflé batter before ultimately screwing up said soufflé anyway. @olivia.adriance's avocado and tomato salad is beautifully simple and a snap to make—you just whisk up a dressing and throw your avo and tomato in there—but it tastes just as good as those pesky recipes that actually require you to put in effort.

HASHTAG PAIRING:
#pureandsimple #avocadolover #flakysaltbae #effortless>effortful

SERVES 4

AVOCADO AND TOMATO SALAD

Olivia Adriance | **@olivia.adriance (oliviaadriance.com)**

¼ cup extra virgin olive oil, plus more for drizzling

Juice of 1 medium lemon (about 2 tablespoons)

1 tablespoon champagne vinegar

1 teaspoon honey

¾ teaspoon grated ginger

Kosher salt and freshly ground black pepper, to taste

2 medium ripe avocados, pitted, peeled, and cut into large dice

1 cup halved grape or cherry tomatoes

¼ cup basil leaves

Flaky sea salt, for finishing

1. In a medium bowl, whisk together the ¼ cup olive oil, lemon juice, vinegar, honey, and ginger. Season with salt and pepper.

2. Add the avocados to the dressing and toss to combine. Cover and set aside at room temperature, 10 to 30 minutes.

3. Just before serving, add the tomatoes and basil and toss. Drizzle with additional olive oil and sprinkle with flaky sea salt.

BUFFALO CHICKEN EGG ROLLS

Brittany Khamille | **@brittany.khamille**

I f you were to make a Tinder account for these Buffalo chicken egg rolls, they would be overloaded with DMs and unsolicited chick pics, because who's going to swipe left on these spicy, crunchy cylinders of beauty? Oozing with melty cheese and Buffalo sauce–coated rotisserie chicken (you could roast your own chicken, but it's a whole lot easier to buy it premade and shred it) this mash-up is made even more irresistible with a homemade ranch dipping sauce. And yeah, you'll probably end up having to block most of the egg rolls' matches because they're asking you to invest in their crypto scams, but that's what you get for making a Tinder account for an appetizer.

HASHTAG PAIRING: #swiperight #chickeninthebuff #mashup #howweroll #foodtinder

MAKES 12 EGG ROLLS; SERVES 6

SAUCE

1 cup mayonnaise

½ cup sour cream

½ cup buttermilk

3 tablespoons chopped chives, plus more for garnish

2 tablespoons chopped dill

2 tablespoons chopped flat-leaf parsley leaves

Cajun seasoning, such as Slap Ya Mama, to taste

ROLLS

2 cups shredded rotisserie chicken

2 (8-ounce) packages shredded pepper jack cheese

8 tablespoons (1 stick) unsalted butter

2 cloves garlic, minced

1 cup hot sauce

2 tablespoons white vinegar

1 teaspoon garlic powder

1 teaspoon onion powder

½ teaspoon white pepper

1 teaspoon Cajun seasoning

1 to 2 quarts vegetable oil, for frying

12 egg roll wrappers

1. MAKE THE RANCH DIPPING SAUCE: In a medium bowl, mix the mayonnaise, sour cream, buttermilk, 3 tablespoons chives, dill, and parsley. Add Cajun seasoning to taste. Cover and refrigerate for at least 30 minutes before serving, or up to 2 weeks in an airtight container.

2. MAKE THE EGG ROLLS: Combine the shredded chicken with the cheese in a medium bowl.

3. Melt the butter in a small saucepan over low heat. Once melted, add the garlic and sauté until fragrant, about 2 minutes. Stir in the hot sauce, vinegar, garlic and onion powders, white pepper, and Cajun seasoning. Taste and adjust the seasoning.

(continued)

4. Pour the mixture over the chicken and cheese and mix until well combined.

5. Place the oil in a large pot and heat to 350°F.

6. Meanwhile, fill a small bowl with water and place near a work surface. Place an egg roll wrapper on the work surface in a diamond shape and put about ⅓ cup of the filling in the middle. Take one corner and fold it into the middle, then tuck in each side. Dip your finger into the water and rub it onto the corner of the wrapper. Roll up the bundle. Repeat with the remaining egg roll wrappers and filling.

7. Once the oil comes to temperature, fry the egg rolls in batches until golden and crispy, about 5 minutes. Remove with a slotted spoon or skimmer and drain briefly on a large plate lined with paper towels. Garnish the dipping sauce with additional chives, and serve the egg rolls hot with the dipping sauce.

Sometimes TikTok doesn't just create trends—it also creates songs. Case in point: the "Eat Your Vegetables" jam, a mash-up of the words of former TikToker That Vegan Teacher with $uicideboy$'s ". . . And to Those I Love, Thanks for Sticking Around." While @nutrition_by_meagan doesn't use the screechy song in her Caesar salad glow-up video (the song is literally a woman shrieking "Eat your vegetables!"), she achieves the difficult task of making us want to not only eat our Brussels sprouts but devour them. The tangy Caesar-like dressing, crunchy chickpeas, and super-crisp sprouts (it's the x carved into each one before baking that does it) are all song-worthy in their own right.

HASHTAG PAIRING:
#brusselssproutsglowup
#saladdays #sproutabouttown
#caesargotmeshook
#eatyourvegetables!

SERVES 2 TO 4

CRISPY BRUSSELS SPROUT "CAESAR" SALAD

Meagan Currell | **@nutrition_by_meagan (nutritionbymeagan.com)**

SALAD

7 ounces (2 cups) brussels sprouts, halved lengthwise

2 tablespoons extra virgin olive oil

1 teaspoon garlic salt

¼ cup shredded Parmesan

¾ cup cooked chickpeas or ½ (15-ounce) can, drained

¼ teaspoon smoked paprika

¼ teaspoon kosher salt

1 slice sourdough bread

1 teaspoon pine nuts

DRESSING

3 tablespoons plain Greek yogurt

1 tablespoon extra virgin olive oil

1 tablespoon minced capers

1 teaspoon Dijon mustard

1 teaspoon grated Parmesan

Juice of ½ medium lemon (about 1 tablespoon)

¼ teaspoon minced garlic

Pinch kosher salt

1. **MAKE THE SALAD:** Preheat the oven to 350°F. Make a small x in the flat side of each sprout with a paring knife.

2. Drizzle 1 tablespoon of the oil, sprinkle ½ teaspoon of the garlic salt, and spread a thin layer of shredded Parmesan (2 to 3 tablespoons) on a large baking sheet lined with parchment paper. Make sure the mixture fully covers the baking sheet. Arrange the brussels sprouts cut sides down on the baking sheet (don't toss them) and bake until the cheese and brussels sprouts are crisp, 25 to 28 minutes.

3. Pat the chickpeas dry and place them on a small baking sheet with 1½ teaspoons of the oil, the paprika, and salt. Roast until golden brown, 20 to 25 minutes.

(continued)

4. Tear the sourdough bread into pieces and place them on a small baking sheet. Add the remaining 1½ teaspoons oil and the remaining ½ teaspoon garlic salt and toss to combine. Bake until crisp and lightly browned, 10 to 12 minutes. (You can cook all of these components at the same time, just stagger the cooking times.)

5. MAKE THE DRESSING: Whisk together the yogurt, oil, capers, mustard, Parmesan, lemon juice, garlic, and salt.

6. Transfer the crispy brussels sprouts to a serving platter, then add the roasted chickpeas and pine nuts. Drizzle with the dressing and top with the croutons and the remaining 1 to 2 tablespoons shredded Parmesan.

There are two things social media loves: a good mash-up and French onion soup (just make it into something other than soup). You've surely heard of the viral French onion pasta (worth the hype), but have you tried French onion soup toasts? If so, TikTok thanks you for giving them all your data, but if you haven't, @saucedupfoods has your new favorite way of eating caramelized alliums.

Besides being an impressive, delicious appetizer, this recipe also costs under twelve dollars to make, and that's if you didn't find your little hunk of Gruyère on sale. It takes all of those sweet, silky flavors from slowly simmered onions and thrusts them upon beautifully crunchy bread. It could very well be the future of French onion anything-but-soup.

HASHTAG PAIRING:
#ISOmorefrenchonion
#toastofthetown #allium?alli-yum!
#ooolala #dontmakeitsoup

MAKES 12 TOASTS;
SERVES 4

FRENCH ONION SOUP BITES

Staley Lane | **@saucedupfoods (saucedupfoods.com)**

2 tablespoons salted butter, plus 2 tablespoons softened

1 large white onion, thinly sliced

2 teaspoons sugar

Leaves of 3 sprigs thyme, chopped, plus more for garnish

3 tablespoons balsamic vinegar

¼ cup low-sodium beef stock, plus more as needed

1 baguette

¾ cup grated Gruyère

1. Melt the 2 tablespoons unsoftened butter in a medium skillet over medium heat and sauté the onion until fragrant, 5 to 7 minutes. Stir in the sugar and chopped thyme.

2. When the onion begins to brown, about 10 additional minutes, add the balsamic vinegar and stock. Cook, stirring occasionally, until the onions are caramelized and most of the liquid has evaporated, 15 to 20 minutes. If the liquid cooks off completely before the onions are caramelized, add beef broth 1 tablespoon at a time to keep the onions from sticking to the pan.

3. Preheat the oven to 500°F and line a large baking sheet with parchment paper. Slice the baguette into twelve ¾-inch-thick pieces. Slather both sides of each piece with the softened butter. Heat a large skillet over medium-high heat and toast the bread slices, 1 to 2 minutes per side.

4. Put the toasted bread on the prepared baking sheet. Top each with some of the caramelized onions and cheese. Bake until the cheese is golden brown and melted, about 6 minutes. Top each with thyme leaves and devour!

L ike waiting for the Starbucks PSL, anticipating @alinaprokuda's annual update to her viral butternut squash soup is becoming a fall rite of passage. When she originally posted the soup in September 2022, the recipe got 40 million views, which is the equivalent of everyone in Canada salivating over this roasted, blended gourd. Her 2023 iteration amps up the heat with Thai chile peppers, but it's the fresh ginger and heavy garlic that really set this bowl apart.

HASHTAG PAIRING: #fallrecipes #itssoupchristmas #ohmygourd #canadalovesthemsomesquash

SERVES 2

BUTTERNUT SQUASH SOUP

Alina Prokuda | **@alinaprokuda**

1 medium butternut squash, peeled, seeded, and cubed

3 carrots, peeled

2 medium shallots, peeled

1 head garlic

2 Thai chile peppers

Extra virgin olive oil, for drizzling

2 teaspoons turmeric

2 teaspoons smoked paprika

Kosher salt and freshly ground black pepper, to taste

1½ cups low-sodium vegetable or chicken broth, plus more if needed

⅓ cup full-fat coconut milk (half 13.5-ounce can), plus more for garnish

1 teaspoon grated ginger

Flat-leaf parsley leaves, croutons, and pumpkin seeds, for garnish

1. Preheat the oven to 375°F. Place the squash, carrots, shallots, garlic, and peppers on a baking sheet.

2. Drizzle olive oil over the vegetables and sprinkle with the turmeric and paprika. Season with salt and pepper. Toss to coat.

3. Bake until the vegetables are golden and easily pierced with a fork, about 45 minutes. Squeeze out the garlic cloves and discard the skin.

4. In a blender, puree the cooked vegetables with the broth, ⅓ cup coconut milk, and ginger until smooth. Transfer to a medium saucepan and reheat gently. Taste and adjust seasoning.

5. Divide the soup between 2 individual serving bowls, and make it pretty by garnishing with parsley, croutons, pumpkin seeds, and a few dots of coconut milk.

A rtichoke recipes just feel special—who eats artichokes on the reg? So when @melissajorealrecipes's stuffed Sicilian-style artichoke recipe appeared on TikTok's FYP, special-craving people gobbled it up, remembering both that 1. Artichokes exist!, and 2. They're insanely easy to make at home. Be sure to get the cheesy, garlicky filling into every little crevice, as you want that stuffing in every bite. And yes, you really do need the full head of garlic, because getting a steamed piece is like winning the lottery, and don't you want that I-won-the-lottery! feeling as much as possible?

HASHTAG PAIRING:
#yayartichokes #openyourheart #garliclottery #okiedokieartichokie

PHOTO TIP: Make the focus go beyond your subject by setting a scene. Add plates, cups, flowers— whatever makes your heart happy.

SERVES 4

STUFFED ARTICHOKES

Melissa Kauper | **@melissajorealrecipes (melissajorealrecipes.com)**

2 lemons

4 globe artichokes

1½ cups Italian-style breadcrumbs

½ cup grated pecorino Romano

Cloves of 1 head garlic, thinly sliced lengthwise

½ cup chopped flat-leaf parsley

½ cup extra virgin olive oil

Kosher salt and freshly ground black pepper, to taste

8 tablespoons (1 stick) unsalted butter, melted, for dipping

1. Squeeze the lemons into a large bowl of cold water and add the spent lemons. Set aside. Cut the stem off each artichoke and slice off the very top so you can open it up. Snip off any brown leaves or pointy tips.

2. Place the trimmed artichokes in the bowl, top sides down, and then run cold water over them to clean them. Remove the artichokes from the water and drain top sides down on paper towels. Remove and reserve squeezed lemons.

3. In a medium bowl combine the breadcrumbs, cheese, about one-quarter of the slivered garlic, the parsley, and ¼ cup of the olive oil. Season with salt and pepper.

4. Gently open up the artichokes and stuff slivered garlic into all the nooks and crannies. Stuff the breadcrumb mixture in between the leaves.

5. Fill a large stockpot with 2 to 3 inches of water so that when you put your artichokes in the pot (open sides up), the water comes about halfway up the artichokes but doesn't flow into the leaves. Place the squeezed lemons in the pot as well. Drizzle the remaining ¼ cup olive oil over the artichokes and season with salt and pepper.

(continued)

6. Bring the water to a boil over high heat, then reduce the heat to low, cover, and steam the artichokes until the leaves pull away easily, about 40 minutes.

7. To enjoy, pull the leaves off, dip in the melted butter, and scrape off the filling with your teeth. Keep going until you get to the heart. Scrape off the fuzzy choke part (not edible), cut the heart into pieces, and dip in the melted butter.

CAJUN CORN RIBS

Carlena Davis | **@spilling_the_sweet_tea (spillingthesweettea.com)**

W hat is it about corn ribs that appeals to our kernel-loving souls? Is it that they're easier to eat than full-on cobs? That they tap into our Cro-Magnon authentic selves? Or maybe that they curl up when cooked to look like cheery little smiles? Whatever the reason, corn ribs have been on social media repeat since @spicednice posted her elote-inspired recipe on TikTok in February 2021. @spilling_the_sweet_tea's take douses them in a beautifully spicy Cajun butter and then doubles down on the Cajun action with a Cajun ranch dip, all of which makes me as excited about corn as the "It's corn!" kid. The hardest part of making corn ribs is cutting them, so please be careful and don't cut off any body parts because I don't need that on my conscience.

HASHTAG PAIRING: #itscorn! #ribsbutmakethemvegetarian #eartoearsmile #cornporn #pleasedontchopoffafinger

SERVES 8

CORN

8 ears corn, shucked

2 sticks (16 tablespoons) salted butter, melted

3 cloves garlic, minced

1 tablespoon Cajun seasoning

1 teaspoon hot sauce

1 teaspoon paprika

Cilantro leaves, for garnish

DIP

¾ cup buttermilk

½ cup mayonnaise

¼ cup sour cream

1 tablespoon Cajun seasoning, plus more for garnish

2 teaspoons dried chives

½ teaspoon dried dill, plus more for garnish

½ teaspoon garlic powder

½ teaspoon onion powder

1. MAKE THE CORN: Cutting the corn can be difficult, and while it may seem counterintuitive, the safest and most efficient way is to first cut off one end so you can stand your corn up vertically. Then take your knife and slice down the middle of the cob. You can also halve the corn crosswise first, so you're working with a shorter piece (they may not curl as well as the full cobs). Either way, keep both hands above the knife. (If your knife isn't super sharp, you'll probably have to pound it down, and if you're still having trouble, try nuking the corn for 20 seconds in the microwave to soften it slightly.) Using the same pound-that-knife-down-the-cob technique, cut each half cob into quarter cobs. Heat a grill to 350°F.

2. Place the melted butter in a small bowl with the garlic, Cajun seasoning, hot sauce, and paprika. Whisk until combined.

3. Brush about three-quarters of the butter mixture onto the corn to cover completely. (Reserve the remaining butter mixture.) Grill, turning occasionally, until the corn is tender enough to pierce with a fork, about 15 minutes.

(continued)

4. **MAKE THE DIP:** In a small bowl, whisk together the buttermilk, mayonnaise, and sour cream until well combined. Whisk in the 1 tablespoon Cajun seasoning, chives, ½ teaspoon dill, and garlic and onion powders. Sprinkle with additional Cajun seasoning and dill. Refrigerate until ready to serve.

5. Using tongs, remove the corn from the grill to a platter and drizzle with the remaining butter mixture. Garnish the corn with cilantro and dip it into that Cajun ranch!

DINNER

BIRRIA TACOS
Dahianna, @_cookingwitd

SPICY VODKA PASTA WITH ITALIAN SAUSAGE
Shakhbazian Otar, @_god_of_food

SMASH BURGERS
Britney Landry, @britscookin

HONEY GARLIC PARMESAN CHICKEN SKEWERS
Carman Wilken, @whatsmomcookin
(whatsmomcookin.com)

MUFFIN TIN SALMON "SUSHI" CUPS
Nicole Keshishian Modic, @kalejunkie
(kalejunkie.com)

CACIO E PEPE PASTA
Ruben Bondi, @cucinaconruben

CAJUN SPICED HONEY GARLIC LOBSTER
David Nguyen, @dvdnguyen
(houseofnguyen.net)

NANA BENEDETTA'S MEATBALLS
Patty and Patty, @pattyandpatty on TikTok,
@pattyandpattynyc on IG (pattyandpatty.com)

BEEF STEW
Barbara Javaid, @barbhomekitchen on
TikTok, @barb.homekitchen on IG

CREAMY LEMON GARLIC CHICKEN WITH GNOCCHI
Sara Haven, @sara.haven

t was the Instagram post heard 'round the world in 2018, when an L.A. influencer posted a picture of his dinner from a neighborhood quesabirria taco truck. Almost instantly, influencers were scouring their own 'hoods for birria tacos, clamoring for that perfect shot of glistening, griddled tacos being dunked into Styrofoam cups full of dark pools of chile-infused goodness. Talk about gussying up #tacotuesday.

Demand skyrocketed, with influencers piquing our interest for a dish that, prior to 2018, was barely known to most outside of Mexico. Birria tacos started popping up on Mexican restaurant menus across the country, and food bloggers began posting recipes for DIY tacos and Frankenfoods like birria ramen. This recipe slow simmers dried guajillo, ancho, and arbol chiles with garlic, onion, oregano, and cumin to out-birria the rest.

HASHTAG PAIRING: #birriatacos #tacotime #whenidipyoudip #tacoboutawesome #birriaiswhyimbroke

PHOTO TIP: With brownish foods like tacos, add pops of color with onion, cilantro, and limes.

SERVES 6

BIRRIA TACOS

Dahianna | **@_cookingwitd**

2 pounds boneless beef chuck roast

6 cloves garlic

5 dried guajillo chiles, stems and seeds removed

5 dried chiles de arbol, stems and seeds removed

4 dried ancho chiles, stems and seeds removed

4 bay leaves

½ medium white onion

½ carrot

1 tablespoon beef or chicken broth

1 tablespoon dried oregano

1 tablespoon ground cumin

1½ teaspoons sugar

1 teaspoon kosher salt

12 yellow corn tortillas

3 cups grated Chihuahua, Oaxaca, or Monterey Jack cheese

Chopped white onion, chopped cilantro, and lime wedges for serving

1. In a large pot or Dutch oven, combine the beef, garlic, chiles, bay leaves, onion, carrot, and 6 cups of water. Bring to a boil over medium heat, then simmer for 30 minutes.

2. With a slotted spoon or skimmer, remove the garlic, chiles, bay leaves, onion, and carrot and place in a blender. Add about ½ cup of cooking liquid and puree. Add the broth, oregano, cumin, sugar, and salt and blend until thoroughly combined. Strain through a fine-mesh sieve back into the pot with the beef and the remaining cooking liquid.

3. Stir to combine, cover, and cook over low heat until the beef shreds with a fork, about 3 hours.

4. Transfer the beef to a cutting board, allow to cool slightly, and shred it with two forks.

5. To make the tacos, heat a cast-iron griddle or skillet over medium-low heat. Dip a corn tortilla halfway into the broth in the pot. Place on the griddle and top with ¼ cup cheese and about

½ cup shredded meat. Add 1 to 2 tablespoons of broth to the griddle, fold the taco, and cook until the cheese melts and the meat sizzles. You can make several tacos at a time.

6. When ready to serve, ladle broth into small individual bowls for dipping and top the broth and the tacos with chopped onion and cilantro. Serve with lime halves on the side.

think more people in America know what Gigi Hadid pasta is than are familiar with the Fourth Amendment, so yeah, that's where we're at, folks. But why worry ourselves with unreasonable search and seizures when there's spicy, creamy, tangy pasta to be eaten? And if you don't trust supermodels with your pasta recipes, look no further than social media's @_god_of_food (aka French private chef Shakhbazian Otar). Out of the approximately two billion online versions of vodka pasta out there, he out-vodkas the rest by adding smoky Calabrian chile peppers and Italian sausage.

HASHTAG PAIRING: #pastafarian #justaddvodka #itreallyisthatgood #infooddeitywetrust #dontseizegigi

SERVES 4

SPICY VODKA PASTA WITH ITALIAN SAUSAGE

Shakhbazian Otar | **@_god_of_food**

1 tablespoon extra virgin olive oil, plus more as needed

1 pound Italian sausage, casings removed

1 small yellow onion, finely diced

3 cloves garlic, sliced

3 tablespoons chopped Calabrian chile pepper

Scant ⅓ cup tomato paste

3 basil leaves

½ cup vodka

1 cup heavy cream, plus more as needed

Kosher salt, to taste

8 ounces dried pappardelle or other dried pasta

1 tablespoon chopped flat-leaf parsley

Grated Parmesan, for serving

1. Warm 1 tablespoon olive oil in a large skillet over medium heat. Add the sausage, use a wooden spoon to break the meat into chunks, and cook until browned. Use a slotted spoon to transfer the sausage from the pan to a plate and set aside.

2. If the pan looks dry, add a bit more olive oil and sauté the onion, garlic, and Calabrian chile pepper until soft, 4 to 5 minutes.

3. Add the tomato paste and basil to the pan and cook for another 2 minutes, stirring occasionally. Stir in the vodka and turn the heat to high. Cook until reduced slightly, 1 to 2 minutes. Meanwhile, bring a large pot of water to a boil for the pasta.

4. Reduce the heat under the skillet to a low simmer and stir in the cream. (If you'd like a super-smooth sauce, you can blend it at this step with an immersion blender or a standard blender, but it's delicious either way.) Return the sausage to the skillet and simmer for 15 minutes.

(continued)

5. Salt the boiling water and cook the pasta until just shy of al dente, according to the package instructions. Reserve 1 cup of the pasta cooking water before draining.

6. Add the pasta and some of the pasta water to the skillet. Toss to combine, then continue cooking until the pasta is al dente, 1 to 2 minutes more, adding more cream or pasta water, if needed. Divide among 4 individual serving plates and scatter on parsley and cheese.

To smash or not to smash? That was the question asked of our burgers over the past few years. Admittedly, I was a holdout on the smash burger front, thinking that smashing the patty would also smash the juices out of it, resulting in a dry, flavorless burger. Oh, my naivete. Smashing the burgers actually locks in the juices while giving them a caramelized, meaty "crust." They're also way faster and easier to make than those mid thick burgers, plus you get to smash something. I'm now a convert, convinced that this is the best way to cook a cheeseburger. @britscookin's version takes it to the next level with bacon, caramelized onions, and a Big Mac–style sauce.

HASHTAG PAIRING:
#smashorpass #bussinburgers #lacybeef #itsthesmashforme #hamletbutmakeitburgers

SERVES 3

SMASH BURGERS

Britney Landry | **@britscookin**

SAUCE

⅓ cup mayonnaise

2 tablespoons yellow mustard

2 tablespoons ketchup

2 teaspoons Worcestershire sauce

2 teaspoons relish

BURGERS

6 slices bacon

1 tablespoon unsalted butter

Kosher salt and freshly ground black pepper, to taste

1 medium yellow onion, coarsely chopped

1 pound (80/20) ground beef

Garlic salt, to taste

6 slices American cheese

3 toasted hamburger buns

1. MAKE THE SAUCE: Mix the mayonnaise, mustard, ketchup, Worcestershire sauce, and relish in a small bowl. Refrigerate until ready to use.

2. MAKE THE BURGERS: Cook the bacon on a griddle over medium heat until crisp. With tongs, remove the bacon to a paper towel–lined plate. Melt the butter with the fat remaining on the griddle, season with salt and pepper, and sauté the onion until it begins to caramelize, about 10 minutes.

3. Divide the beef into six equal pieces and roll each into a ball. When the onions are starting to caramelize, transfer them to a bowl. (Don't worry if a few remain behind.) Increase the heat to high. Making sure you have plenty of room, place 2 to 3 balls of beef on the griddle and get to smashing. To smash, use a dedicated burger press or a heavy cast-iron skillet—just be sure to place a piece of parchment paper or aluminum foil between the smasher and the meat so the beef doesn't stick to the smasher. Press down firmly to get the burgers really thin.

(continued)

4. Season the smashed beef with garlic salt and pepper and cook for 2 minutes.

5. Flip the burgers with a large spatula. Add some onions on top of each burger. Top with about 1 tablespoon of the prepared sauce and 1 slice American cheese. Cook until the cheese is melted, 1 to 2 minutes.

6. Remove the burgers from the heat and repeat until all the burgers are cooked. Build those perfect smash burgers by loading up each toasted bun with 2 to 3 patties. Top with additional onions, the bacon, and additional sauce.

can't explain why recipes for chicken skewers went viral. It could be because people just love food on a stick, or maybe everyone got an air fryer for Christmas and was desperate to use it more than once. (This recipe can be made with or without an air fryer.) But in 2022 and 2023, every food influencer worth their baked feta pasta was making and posting recipes for chicken skewers. @whatsmomcookin's version is slightly sweet and exceedingly juicy, and made even better by a generous slathering of garlic butter applied just before serving.

HASHTAG PAIRING:
#kindakebabs #chickenrecipe #longpointedobjects #thighgap #kitchenknivesandskewwwwers

PHOTO TIP: Try different angles when shooting. Start with an overhead, sure, but also try straight-on and three-quarter orientations so you have options when choosing the best photo of the dish.

SERVES 2 TO 4

HONEY GARLIC PARMESAN CHICKEN SKEWERS

Carman Wilken | **@whatsmomcookin (whatsmomcookin.com)**

½ cup extra virgin olive oil

¾ cup freshly grated Parmesan

8 to 9 cloves garlic, minced

4 tablespoons honey

2 teaspoons smoked paprika

2 teaspoons onion powder

1 teaspoon dried oregano

½ teaspoon red pepper flakes

Juice of 1 medium lemon (about 2 tablespoons)

Kosher salt and freshly ground black pepper, to taste

2 pounds boneless, skinless chicken thighs, cut into bite-size pieces

4 to 5 tablespoons salted butter, softened

1 tablespoon dried parsley

1. In a medium bowl, whisk together the olive oil, ½ cup of the Parmesan, 5 to 6 cloves of the minced garlic, 2 tablespoons of the honey, the paprika, onion powder, oregano, red pepper flakes, and lemon juice. Season with salt and pepper and add the chicken. Toss to coat thoroughly, and marinate in the refrigerator for at least 1 hour and up to 12 hours.

2. Preheat the oven to 350°F or an air fryer to 400°F.

3. Thread 6 to 8 pieces of marinated chicken on a metal skewer, packing them fairly tightly. Repeat with the remaining chicken. (You can use wooden skewers, but they need to be soaked in water for 30 minutes first.)

(continued)

4. If cooking in the oven, place the skewers on a baking sheet and bake for 15 to 17 minutes, then flip and cook until the chicken reaches an internal temperature of 165°F, 5 to 8 additional minutes. In the air fryer, cook for 12 minutes, then flip and cook until the chicken reaches an internal temperature of 165°F, 5 to 7 additional minutes.

5. In a small bowl, mix the butter with the remaining 3 cloves minced garlic, the remaining 2 tablespoons honey, the remaining ¼ cup Parmesan, and the parsley. Brush this mixture all over the chicken and serve hot on the skewers.

nstead of asking why TikTok is obsessed with cooking non-muffin-foods in muffin tins, we should really be asking ourselves why we aren't using this back-of-the-cabinet kitchen pan more often. Why relegate this perfectly sized portion maker to muffins when there's a wide world of foods just begging to be baked in a muffin tin?

Intrigued by the muffin tin trend, I decided to eat all of my meals for a day cooked from muffin tins. Muffin tin egg cups, muffin tin tacos, muffin tin cakes; but my favorite muffin tin food—the one I'd eat regardless of whether I had a weird resolution to theme my meals around muffin tins—was muffin tin sushi. Handheld, reasonably healthy, and so tasty, @kalejunkie's take on the trend is so good that you might start referring to your muffin tin as your sushi cup tin.

HASHTAG PAIRING: #muffintinday #sushicups #haveariceday #renamemuffintins

PHOTO TIP: If your recipe includes something interesting, like, say, a muffin tin, try to work it into your photo. By showing special props and the finished recipe, you're telling a complete story.

MAKES 12 PIECES; SERVES 4

MUFFIN TIN SALMON "SUSHI" CUPS

Nicole Keshishian Modic | **@kalejunkie (kalejunkie.com)**

Nonstick cooking spray, for pan

1½ pounds skinless salmon, cut into 1-inch cubes

2 tablespoons soy sauce or coconut aminos

2 tablespoons Kewpie mayonnaise, plus more for serving

1 pinch kosher salt

1½ cups cooked sushi rice

1 teaspoon unseasoned rice vinegar

3 large sheets nori, cut into 12 (4-inch) squares

1 tablespoon sesame seeds

2 scallions, chopped

1. Preheat the oven to 400°F and lightly coat a standard-size muffin tin with nonstick cooking spray.

2. In a large bowl, combine the salmon, soy sauce, 2 tablespoons mayonnaise, and salt. Toss to combine.

3. In a separate medium bowl, combine the rice and vinegar. Toss to combine.

4. Place a nori square on a work surface and put 2 to 3 tablespoons rice in the center. Place the nori and filling in a muffin tin indentation, gently molding it to fit. Repeat with the remaining nori and rice.

5. Top each nori cup with about 2 tablespoons of the salmon mixture. Bake the cups until the salmon is pink and flaky, about 15 minutes. To serve, top each cup with a squeeze of mayonnaise, a sprinkle of sesame seeds, and some scallion.

For @cucinaconruben's first English-language TikTok video, he chose a classic from his home city of Rome. Since he has lived and breathed Internet-favorite cacio e pepe his entire life, he is the man we should be listening to when it comes to making it. His tips: Don't disgrace the pasta with butter and cream. Use a short noodle, like rigatoni or mezze maniche. The sauce should not be so creamy that it slides off the noodle. (No, it must cling to the rigatoni like America clings to the two-party political system.) Always use high-quality cheese. And finally, zest a little lemon (go organic since you're using the peel) over the top to brighten it up.

HASHTAG PAIRING: #sendnoods #cheesycomecheesygo #cacioepepe4president #noreallycacioepepe4president

SERVES 4

CACIO E PEPE PASTA

Ruben Bondi | **@cucinaconruben**

Kosher salt, to taste

8 ounces short dried pasta, such as rigatoni or mezze maniche

1 to 2 tablespoons whole black peppercorns

Extra virgin olive oil, for drizzling

1 heaping cup (good-quality!) finely grated pecorino Romano, plus more for serving (use a Microplane)

Finely grated organic lemon zest, for serving

1. Bring a large pot of water to a boil. Once boiling, add salt and the pasta. While the pasta cooks, grind the peppercorns. Put the ground pepper in a large skillet over low heat. Toast the pepper until fragrant, 20 to 30 seconds.

2. Add a drizzle of olive oil and 1 cup water to the skillet with the pepper. Cook the mixture to create an emulsion.

3. When the pasta is almost al dente, reserve 1 cup of the pasta cooking water and then drain the pasta. Add the pasta to the skillet with ¼ cup of the cooking water. Stir with a large spoon. Cook until creamy, 2 to 3 additional minutes. (The secret is to make the pasta creamy before adding the cheese.)

4. Turn off the heat and wait at least 30 seconds and up to a few minutes—the pasta's temperature must drop or the cheese will split and the sauce won't be creamy. Incorporate the grated cheese (the finer the shred, the easier it will melt) in 3 additions, alternating with a bit of pasta water and stirring between additions. At first the consistency may be pasty, but gradually it will become creamy. Top with grated lemon zest and more grated cheese, and enjoy immediately while it's still hot!

A single lobster tail? A total treat. A duo of lobster tails? Hyper-indulgent. But five lobster tails? That's some gangsta-level living right there. @dvdnguyen is clearly making exceptional life decisions, and his Cajun spiced lobster is the antidote you need to your non-five-lobster-tail life.

Drizzled with a kicky, buttery blend of Cajun spices and lemon pepper—plus honey and lemon juice to amp up the flavor even more—and you'll understand why every time @dvdnguyen cooks with shellfish the result becomes TikTok gold.

HASHTAG PAIRING:
#notamollusk #fancyeats #spicylobstersdoitbetter #crustaceanonyou

SERVES 4

CAJUN SPICED HONEY GARLIC LOBSTER

David Nguyen | **@dvdnguyen (houseofnguyen.net)**

5 lobster tails, each halved lengthwise then crosswise into quarters

8 tablespoons (1 stick) salted butter

Kosher salt and freshly ground black pepper, to taste

6 cloves garlic, minced

2 teaspoons Cajun seasoning

1 teaspoon lemon pepper seasoning

1 teaspoon paprika

¼ cup plus 2 tablespoons honey

Juice of 2 medium lemons (¼ cup), plus lemon wedges for garnish

4 scallions, cut lengthwise into thin strands

1. Preheat the oven to 400°F. Nestle the quartered lobster tails in a 10-inch baking dish or cast-iron skillet.

2. Melt 3 tablespoons of the butter and drizzle it over the lobster. Season with salt and pepper. Bake the lobster until the meat is white, firm, and cooked through, 14 to 15 minutes.

3. While the lobsters bake, melt the remaining 5 tablespoons butter in a small skillet over medium-low heat. Add the minced garlic and cook until fragrant, 1 to 2 minutes.

4. Add the Cajun seasoning, lemon pepper, and paprika, stir with a wooden spoon, and allow the spices to toast, 5 to 8 minutes.

5. Stir in the honey and lemon juice.

6. Drizzle the sauce over the cooked lobster. Garnish with scallions and lemon wedges and serve from the baking dish. Indulge!

Patty and Patty watching ridiculous TikTok food trends on their web series are all of us. They gasp in horror as a blonde pours a Barbie-pink, smoothie-esque sauce over her pasta; they cringe when a guy inexplicably deep-fries a pizza; and they visibly recoil when someone uses—gasp!—tomato sauce straight from the jar. To set us straight on what Italian food should really taste like, the ladies gave us a recipe for one of social media's early food obsessions: meatballs. Nana Benedetta's spheres are packed with garlic, onion, fresh parsley, and Parmesan before hitting an olive oil–coated skillet. Just don't pour a jar of store-bought sauce over them.

HASHTAG PAIRING: #comfortfood #ditchthejar #havesomeballs #pleasedontputsmoothiesonpasta

SERVES 4

NANA BENEDETTA'S MEATBALLS

Patty and Patty | @pattyandpatty on TikTok | @pattyandpattynyc on IG (pattyandpatty.com)

1 pound ground beef or a combo of beef, pork, and veal

3 cloves garlic, minced

1 small yellow onion, finely diced (about ½ cup)

1 large egg

½ cup seasoned Italian breadcrumbs

¼ cup grated Parmesan, plus more for serving

¼ cup chopped flat-leaf parsley

¼ teaspoon red pepper flakes

Kosher salt and freshly ground black pepper, to taste

1 tablespoon extra virgin olive oil

Homemade marinara sauce, for serving

1. In a large bowl, use your hands or a large spoon to combine the beef, garlic, onion, egg, breadcrumbs, ¼ cup Parmesan, parsley, and red pepper flakes. Season with salt and pepper.

2. Roll the mixture into balls (you choose the size). Heat a large skillet over medium-high and add the olive oil. Brown the meatballs on one side, 4 to 5 minutes. Turn and cook on the other side until they are cooked through and the internal temperature registers 160° to 165°F, 4 to 5 additional minutes. Place on a serving dish, top with some sauce, and sprinkle with more cheese. You can also simmer the meatballs in sauce for at least 45 minutes and up to as long as you've got! (The longer they cook, the better they taste.)

When you think of sexy foods, beef stew probably doesn't come to mind. It's brown, it's halfway between a soup and a meal, and yet it's somehow very, very popular with millions of social media users. Blame it on #soupseason or just a yearning for comfort in our less-than-comfortable world, but beef stew recipes are Instagram and TikTok gold. This version from @barbhomekitchen is why: it's easy to prepare and full of rich, layered flavors. It's the beef stew that will never, ever ghost you, call you crazy, or lead you on for eight months and introduce you to its mother before saying it doesn't really want anything serious. On second thought, beef stew is pretty sexy.

HASHTAG PAIRING:
#meatandpotatoes #theotherstew #unsexyisthenewsexy #beefstewdontghost

SERVES 4

BEEF STEW

Barbara Javaid | **@barbhomekitchen on TikTok** | **@barb.homekitchen on IG**

2 tablespoons all-purpose flour

1 teaspoon smoked paprika

1 teaspoon red pepper flakes

½ teaspoon kosher salt

Pinch freshly ground black pepper

2 pounds chuck roast, cut into bite-size pieces

3 tablespoons extra virgin olive oil

2 medium yellow onions, coarsely chopped

2 cloves garlic, minced

1 tablespoon tomato paste

4½ cups low-sodium beef broth or beef bouillon with water

2 carrots, chopped into bite-size pieces

2 Yukon gold or other waxy potatoes, peeled and chopped into 1-inch chunks

Chopped flat-leaf parsley, for garnish

Crusty bread, for serving

1. Mix the flour, paprika, red pepper flakes, salt, and pepper in a large bowl. Add the beef and toss to coat.

2. Heat 2 tablespoons of the olive oil in a Dutch oven or other large pot over medium-high heat. Add the beef and cook, turning occasionally, until just starting to brown on all sides, 5 to 7 minutes. With a slotted spoon, remove the beef to a plate or bowl and set aside.

3. Reduce the heat to medium-low and add the remaining 1 tablespoon oil to the pot. Add the onions and garlic and sauté until softened, about 4 minutes.

4. Stir in the tomato paste, then pour in the beef broth. Return the beef to the pot, along with any collected juices, and give it a good stir. Cover and simmer for 1 hour 15 minutes.

5. Add the carrots and potatoes, cover, and cook until the carrots, potatoes, and beef are fork-tender, 30 to 40 additional minutes. Ladle into serving bowls, garnish with parsley, and serve with crusty bread.

You've probably heard of Marry Me Chicken—how could you not, as the creamy, sautéed chicken dish was Google's most searched recipe in 2022. But have you heard of what I'm dubbing Just Hang Out and Be Respectful and Leave at a Reasonable Time Chicken? Because that might be even better than that ball-and-chain bird, especially since this chicken involves kicky lemon pepper seasoning, lemon juice, and gnocchi. Sure, @sara.haven's chicken dish could inspire someone to put a ring on it (if that's what you're looking for), but it's also great as a just-for-some-companionship meal while we get through this weird time, you know?

 # HASHTAG PAIRING:
#chickendinner
#allthesingleladies #lemon>ring
#readyorgnocchhereicome

SERVES 4

CREAMY LEMON GARLIC CHICKEN WITH GNOCCHI

Sara Haven | **@sara.haven**

12 ounces to 1 pound boneless, skinless chicken breasts, halved lengthwise to make cutlets

1 teaspoon lemon pepper seasoning

¾ teaspoon garlic powder

2 tablespoons extra virgin olive oil or unsalted butter

3 cloves garlic, minced

½ cup low-sodium chicken or vegetable broth, plus more if needed

Juice of ½ medium lemon (1 tablespoon)

1 cup heavy cream (or plant-based cream)

1 pound potato gnocchi

⅓ cup grated Parmesan

3 cups fresh baby spinach

Lemon slices, for garnish

1. Season both sides of the chicken cutlets with the lemon pepper seasoning and garlic powder.

2. Heat the olive oil in a large skillet over medium-high heat. Add the garlic and sauté until fragrant, 2 to 3 minutes. Put the chicken in the skillet and cook until golden brown and cooked through, about 5 minutes per side. Transfer the chicken to a plate.

3. Add the broth and lemon juice to the skillet and stir. Stir in the cream and gnocchi, making sure the gnocchi are covered in sauce; if necessary, add more broth to cover. Simmer, uncovered, stirring occasionally, until the sauce has thickened and the gnocchi are cooked, 5 to 7 minutes.

4. Remove the pan from the heat and add the cheese and spinach. Toss until the spinach is wilted. Return the chicken cutlets to the skillet and give everything a stir. Let the chicken warm up for 1 to 2 minutes, then garnish with lemon slices and serve.

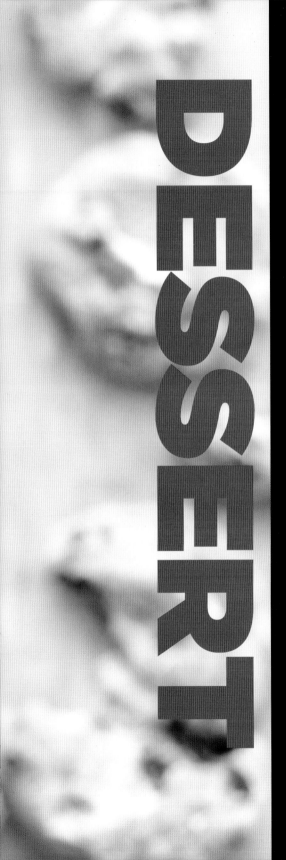

DESSERT

COSMIC BROWNIES
Tessa Arias, @handletheheat
(handletheheat.com)

RED VELVET CUPCAKE COOKIES
Chahinez Tabet Aoul, @thelifestyleofafoodie on
TikTok, @chahinez_tbt on IG (lifestyleofafoodie.com)

DALGONA COFFEE CHOCOLATE CAKE
Kimberlee Ho, @kickassbaker
(kickassbaker.com)

BROWN BUTTER RICE KRISPIE TREATS
Lynja, @cookingwithlynja

CARAMEL APPLE BARK
Garianne Sheridan, @gariannestable
(gariannestable.com)

NO-BAKE BRÛLÉE CHEESECAKES
Chloe Huang, @its.chloeh

S'MORES COOKIES
Tiff's Treats, @tiffstreats

Social media loves everything from the 1990s and 2000s, probably because TikTok's and Instagram's core users are millennials and Gen Zers, nostalgic for times of tech busts, Y2K fears, and unwrapping Little Debbie treats packed in their school lunches. And the king of all bag-lunch treats were Cosmic Brownies. Fudgy, dense, and topped with break-your-teeth rainbow-colored candy spheres, Little Debbie outdid herself when the product debuted in 1999. @handletheheat has made an even better version that will take you right back to the turn of the millennium, minus all the Y2K hysteria.

HASHTAG PAIRING:
#browniebrigade #munchies #lildebbie4eva #lineornoline? #tellmeyouwereborninthe90s withouttellingmeyouwere borninthe90s

PHOTO TIP: For recipes that make a batch, like brownies and cookies, use those multiples to your advantage, taking photographs with all of them or lining up the prettiest. And remember, if the photo makes you hungry, you're doing it right!

MAKES 16 BROWNIES

COSMIC BROWNIES

Tessa Arias | **@handletheheat (handletheheat.com)**

Cooking spray, for pan

10 tablespoons (1¼ sticks) unsalted butter

1 cup granulated sugar

¾ cup plus 2 tablespoons unsweetened cocoa powder, sifted

⅓ cup packed light brown sugar

2 large eggs plus 1 egg yolk

1 tablespoon corn syrup

½ teaspoon vanilla extract

⅔ cup all-purpose flour

1 tablespoon cornstarch

¼ teaspoon kosher salt

½ cup heavy cream

1½ cups semisweet chocolate chips

Wilton Rainbow Chip Crunch, mini M&Ms, sprinkles, or other candy, for topping

1. Preheat the oven to 350°F. Line an 8-inch square metal baking pan with parchment or foil and spray with cooking spray.

2. In a large, microwave-safe bowl, melt the butter for about 90 seconds on high power. Stir in the granulated sugar, cocoa powder, and brown sugar. If still very hot, let cool slightly before adding the eggs and egg yolk, corn syrup, and vanilla. Stir until very well combined.

3. Stir in the flour, cornstarch, and salt until just combined. The batter will be thick. Pour into the prepared pan and bake for 25 minutes. Let cool completely in the pan.

4. To make the frosting, pour the cream into a small microwave-safe bowl and microwave on high for 1 minute. Add the chocolate chips. Let stand for 3 minutes, then stir until smooth.

5. Pour the frosting over the cooled brownies and spread evenly with a spatula. Sprinkle with the candy. Refrigerate until the frosting is set, 1 to 2 hours, before cutting. The brownies can be stored in an airtight container for 3 days at room temperature and for up to 1 week in the fridge. The brownies are best served chilled.

A lot happened in 2008. It was the year that Facebook hit 100 million users, and it was the year that I've deemed peak red velvet. You couldn't waddle down a grocery store aisle without being assaulted with red velvet potato chips, red velvet bagels, and red velvet KitKats. And while we as a culture should probably stop with red velvet everything, these cupcake cookies should not be stopped, and should instead be encouraged to flourish and spawn and create as many red cookies as possible.

@thelifestyleofafoodie's version gives us all the buttery, chocolatey goodness we seek from red velvet, with a healthy heaping of red food coloring. (Use the gel kind to achieve an especially vibrant scarlet.) She crowns her crimson cookies with tangy cream cheese frosting and more cookie crumbs. Your kitchen will smell so good that you won't need your mid-2000s red velvet cupcake candle.

MAKES 9 LARGE COOKIES

HASHTAG PAIRING:
#redvelveteverything #tbt #frostyocookies #makeitred #notredvelvetfriedchicken

RED VELVET CUPCAKE COOKIES

Chahinez Tabet Aoul | **@thelifestyleofafoodie on TikTok** | **@chahinez_tbt on IG (lifestyleofafoodie.com)**

COOKIES

8 tablespoons (1 stick) unsalted butter, softened

⅔ cup brown sugar

½ cup granulated sugar

1 large egg

1 teaspoon vanilla extract

1 teaspoon white vinegar

1 to 2 teaspoons red gel food coloring

1¾ cups all-purpose flour

¼ cup cocoa powder

2 tablespoons cornstarch

½ teaspoon baking powder

¼ teaspoon kosher salt

FROSTING

4 ounces cream cheese, softened

3 tablespoons unsalted butter, softened

1 cup confectioners' sugar

1 teaspoon vanilla extract

1. **MAKE THE COOKIES:** Preheat the oven to 350°F. Line a baking sheet with parchment paper.

2. In a large bowl, cream the butter and sugars together with a large spoon until smooth and creamy.

3. Whisk in the egg, vanilla, vinegar, and food coloring until combined.

4. Mix in the flour, cocoa powder, cornstarch, baking powder, and salt with a large spoon until the flour just disappears; don't overmix the dough. Set aside 1 tablespoon of cookie dough.

5. Using a large cookie scoop (or an ice cream scoop or large spoon), scoop out 9 equal-size cookie dough balls. Place them on the prepared baking sheet and gently flatten them to about ½ inch thick. Bake the cookies for 10 minutes, then let them cool on the baking sheet for 10 to 15 minutes before transferring to a rack to cool completely.

(continued)

6. Bake the 1 tablespoon of reserved dough for 7 to 8 minutes. (You can bake it at the same time as the others, but remove it earlier. When it is cool, crumble it and set the crumbs aside.)

7. **MAKE THE CREAM CHEESE FROSTING:** In a stand mixer fitted with the paddle attachment, or with an electric hand mixer and a large bowl, cream the softened cream cheese and butter until smooth and fluffy, about 3 minutes. Add the confectioners' sugar and vanilla and beat until fluffy, 3 to 5 minutes. (If the frosting seems soft, chill it in the fridge for a few minutes and then beat it again.)

8. Place the frosting in a piping bag fitted with a large smooth tip (or in a zip-top bag with the corner cut off) and frost each cookie. Top with the cookie crumbs.

Remember early in the pandemic when we all vigorously whisked instant coffee and water, because it was better than facing the harrowing reality that our lives were forever changed for the worse? With nowhere to go, we figured why not beef up our forearms and post about it on social like everyone else in the world was doing, after Korean actor Jung Il-Woo coined the whipped coffee dalgona in early 2020. (Because it tasted like the Korean honeycomb candy called dalgona.)

This recipe takes our spring-fling quarantine dalgona coffee and makes it cake. And not just any cake, but the moistest chocolate cake you've ever had, plus a frothy/sweet frosting. Because everything goes down easier in chocolate cake form, even deadly global pandemics.

HASHTAG PAIRING:
#dalgonacoffeechallenge
#cakesofinstagram #cakebuzz
#quarantinethrowback
#cakeorcovid?

SERVES 10 TO 12

DALGONA COFFEE CHOCOLATE CAKE

Kimberlee Ho | **@kickassbaker (kickassbaker.com)**

CAKE

2 sticks (16 tablespoons) unsalted butter, softened, plus more for pans

1½ cups all-purpose flour, plus 1 tablespoon for pans

1 cup unsweetened cocoa powder

1 cup hot brewed coffee

½ cup full-fat sour cream

1 teaspoon vanilla extract

1 cup granulated sugar

½ cup packed light brown sugar

3 large eggs, at room temperature

1 teaspoon baking soda

1 teaspoon kosher salt

FROSTING

½ cup granulated sugar

¼ cup instant coffee granules

¼ cup boiling water

1 cup heavy cream

½ cup mascarpone, stirred until smooth

1 tablespoon confectioners' sugar

1. MAKE THE CAKE: Preheat the oven to 350°F. Butter two 8-inch round cake pans. Divide the 1 tablespoon flour between the pans, tapping the sides of each pan while tilting it slowly in a circle to spread the flour evenly over the butter. Tip each pan over the sink to tap out any excess flour. Set aside.

2. In a medium bowl, whisk together the cocoa powder, brewed coffee, sour cream, and vanilla. Set aside.

3. In the bowl of a stand mixer fitted with the paddle attachment, beat the 2 sticks butter until smooth and shiny, 2 to 3 minutes. Add the granulated and brown sugars and continue beating until fluffy, another 2 to 3 minutes, then beat in the eggs, one at a time, mixing well between each addition.

4. In a small bowl, whisk together the 1½ cups flour, baking soda, and salt. Add one-third of the flour mixture to the butter mixture and beat on low speed until just incorporated. Add one-third of the cocoa mixture and beat until just incorporated. Add the flour and cocoa mixtures in two more additions each, alternating them, until everything is just incorporated. Scrape down the sides of the bowl with a spatula a few times.

5. Divide the batter evenly between the prepared cake pans and bake until a toothpick inserted in the center of the cakes comes out clean and the edges are just starting to pull away from the sides of the pans, 25 to 28 minutes. Let the cakes cool in their pans for 10 minutes, then turn them out onto a wire rack to cool completely before frosting.

6. MAKE THE FROSTING: In the clean bowl of a stand mixer fitted with the whisk attachment, combine the granulated sugar, instant coffee, and boiling water. Whisk by hand until the mixture begins to thicken a little and gets frothy and increases in volume, 30 to 60 seconds. Switch to whisking with the stand mixer at medium to high speed until stiff peaks form and the mixture is a light brown color, 1 to 2 minutes. Use a rubber spatula to transfer to a clean bowl and set aside.

7. Wipe out the stand mixer bowl and clean the whisk attachment, then whisk the heavy cream, mascarpone, and confectioners' sugar at low speed. Gradually increase the speed until the mixture is light and fluffy, 1 to 2 minutes.

8. Scrape the whipped coffee mixture into the whipped mascarpone mixture and whisk on medium speed to combine evenly, 30 to 60 seconds.

9. When the cakes are completely cool, level them by trimming the domed tops off with a serrated knife or cake leveler. Place the first layer on a large plate or cake stand and frost with about half of the coffee frosting. Top with the second cake layer and frost the top with the remaining frosting. Slice and eat!

Lynja was TikTok's favorite cooking grandma. With video editing and splicing that would make a twenty-year-old jealous, the retired-MIT-engineer-turned-TikTok-and-YouTube-star proved that not all influencers are young blondes with a propensity for oversize cardigans. Her quirky videos featured accessible recipes, lots of green-screen action, and cameos by little Lynja cheering herself on (or dancing or yelling at her to stir faster). Lynja passed away in early 2024, but her legacy lives on in so many ways, including these brown butter Rice Krispie treats that were her favorite late-night snack.

HASHTAG PAIRING:
#snapcracklepop
#teambrownbutter
#sponsormekelloggs
#sexagenariansdoitbetter
#weloveyoulynja

PHOTO TIP: Cheese pull, who? You can also get a great pull shot by slowly stretching apart these gooey marshmallow treats.

MAKES 12 SQUARES

BROWN BUTTER RICE KRISPIE TREATS

Lynja | **@cookingwithlynja**

2 sticks (16 tablespoons) unsalted butter, plus more for pan

2 (10-ounce) bags mini marshmallows

1 teaspoon vanilla extract

¾ teaspoon kosher salt

1 (12-ounce box; 10 to 12 cups) puffed rice cereal

1. Butter a 9 x 13-inch baking pan. Melt the 2 sticks butter in a large stainless steel pot over medium-low heat. Cook the butter low and slow, swirling it around occasionally as it becomes golden and pops. After 5 to 8 minutes, it should develop a nutty aroma and turn a toasty brown.

2. Add the marshmallows, vanilla, and salt. Reduce the heat to low and stir constantly until the marshmallows melt. Remove the pot from the heat.

3. Add the cereal and stir with a wooden spoon or rubber spatula until it is thoroughly coated with the marshmallow mixture. Gently press the mixture into the prepared baking pan in an even layer. Cool to room temperature (about 1 hour), then cut and serve.

Candy bark has been around forever (or maybe not forever, but why wouldn't cavemen melt down some cacao beans and throw in something crunchy?), but you probably didn't take notice until recently. Why? Because Instagram didn't exist until 2010. It wasn't until our great food trend disseminator came about that we got to know, love, and post pictures of our bark creations. Now we're all about that bark because it's super easy to make and endlessly customizable, and you literally get to break it!

@gariannestable's caramel apple bark went viral in 2022, and not just because all of us basic Bs jump at any excuse to screech, "It's fall, y'all!" Eating this salty (thanks to the pretzels), chocolatey, caramelly, appley treat in a flat version is way easier than losing a filling biting into an actual caramel apple. You can use any type of apple you'd like, but squeeze a little lemon juice over the pieces to prevent them from browning.

HASHTAG PAIRING:
#breakmybark #2Ddesserts
#keepyourteeth
#youcouldevenuseahammer

MAKES 1 (10 BY 12-INCH) SHEET OF BARK; SERVES 4 TO 6

CARAMEL APPLE BARK

Garianne Sheridan | @gariannestable (gariannestable.com)

1 to 2 Granny Smith or other apples

Juice of ½ medium lemon (1 tablespoon)

6 ounces milk chocolate chips (dark and white chocolate also work)

2 cups small-size salted pretzels, or enough to cover the chocolate surface

1 cup caramel sauce

1. Core and chop the apples (but leave the peel on). Place the pieces in a large bowl and sprinkle with lemon juice to prevent browning.

2. Line a rimmed baking sheet at least 10 by 12 inches with parchment paper. Melt the chocolate chips in a small saucepan over low heat on the stovetop, or in a microwave-safe bowl at 30-second intervals in the microwave. Spread all but about 1 tablespoon of the melted chocolate over the parchment into a 10 by 12–inch rectangle.

3. Scatter pretzels in an even layer on the surface of the chocolate.

4. Place the caramel sauce in a microwave-safe bowl and microwave for about 20 seconds, then spread all but about 1 tablespoon over the pretzels.

5. Top with the apple pieces. Drizzle the reserved chocolate and caramel over the bark. Freeze until hardened, at least 2 hours. To serve, break with a clean hammer (fun way) or chef's knife (more normal way). Store leftovers in an airtight container in the freezer.

NO-BAKE BRÛLÉE CHEESECAKES

Chloe Huang | **@its.chloeh**

8 graham crackers

6 tablespoons unsalted butter, melted

2 heaping tablespoons dark brown sugar

Finely grated zest of ½ organic lemon, plus 2 teaspoons lemon juice

⅔ cup heavy cream

10 ounces cream cheese, softened

⅔ cup confectioners' sugar

2 teaspoons vanilla extract

¼ cup plus 2 tablespoons granulated sugar

1. Crush the graham crackers into crumbs. (Use a food processor fitted with the metal blade or place them in a zip-top bag and crush them manually with a pestle or rolling pin.) In a small bowl, use a spatula to combine the cracker crumbs, melted butter, brown sugar, and lemon zest.

2. Divide the mixture among six 6-ounce ramekins. Press into the bottoms to form a solid base. Place the ramekins in the fridge.

3. In a medium bowl, whip the cream with an electric mixer on high speed until soft peaks form. Set aside.

4. In a large bowl, beat the cream cheese with an electric mixer until smooth. Add the confectioners' sugar, lemon juice, and vanilla. Whisk until smooth.

5. With a spatula, fold in the whipped cream until it's homogenous. Divide the mixture among the ramekins and smooth the tops. Refrigerate for at least 1 hour to set. (Or cover and refrigerate for up to 3 days.)

6. When ready to serve, sprinkle 1 tablespoon granulated sugar on the surfaces of each. Using a kitchen torch, melt the sugar until it caramelizes. (You can also broil them in the oven if you don't have a kitchen torch. Preheat the broiler and place the ramekins on a baking sheet. Broil until the sugar is golden, 5 to 10 minutes, keeping an eye on them. Let them cool slightly before continuing.) Refrigerate until the sugar hardens, at least 30 minutes. Grab a spoon and crack open!

don't know which was bigger in the summer of 2023, these s'mores cookies or the Taylor Swift Eras tour. Both are gorgeous creations out of our wildest dreams that have a bit of a naughty reputation, and all through August both had girls shaking it off and screaming with glee. There's no reason to cheat with store-bought cookie dough when you know all too well that this chocolate chip cookie recipe from @tiffstreats is so easy, and about 1,989 times tastier. Don't blame me when you eat the whole batch fresh from the oven, all warm and gooey—for you and these cookies it's a love story, baby, just say, "Yes."

HASHTAG PAIRING:
#lookwhatyoumademedo #s'moreplease #imthecookieitsme #wishitmade22

PHOTO TIP: Use random, fun props you have at home, like these magnetic tiles from a word game. If you can't surround cookies with words like "fantasy" and "nibble" on social media, where can you?

MAKES 14 COOKIES

S'MORES COOKIES

Tiff's Treats | **@tiffstreats**

2¼ sticks (18 tablespoons) salted butter, softened

1 cup granulated sugar

½ cup firmly packed light brown sugar

2 large eggs

2 teaspoons vanilla extract

1½ teaspoons kosher salt

½ teaspoon baking soda

2¼ cups all-purpose flour

1 (12-ounce) package semisweet chocolate chips

7 whole graham crackers, broken in half to make 14 squares

1 king-size (2.6-ounce) Hershey's chocolate bar, broken into 14 squares

14 marshmallows

1. Preheat the oven to 375°F. Line two baking sheets with parchment paper. In a large bowl, cream the butter and granulated and brown sugars using an electric mixer on medium speed until the mixture is smooth, 2 to 3 minutes.

2. Add the eggs, vanilla, salt, and baking soda. Mix on medium speed until the ingredients are incorporated and smooth, 2 to 3 minutes.

3. Add the flour. Mix on low speed until the flour is partially incorporated, then on medium speed until fully incorporated. Stir in the chocolate chips with a large spoon until incorporated fully.

4. Place 7 graham cracker squares on each sheet, at least 2 inches apart. Top each cracker with a square of chocolate. Place a marshmallow on top of the chocolate on each.

5. Scoop about ⅓ cup of the cookie dough and flatten it with your fingers so you can mold it around the marshmallow without smooshing it. The dough should cover the marshmallow and most of the cracker. Repeat with the remaining dough.

6. Bake until the cookie edges are brown and set, 11 to 13 minutes. Let the cookies sit for 1 minute so they won't crumble when transferred, then remove them to cool on a wire rack. Serve warm for maximum gooeyness.

DRINKS

LYCHEE MINT BUBBLE TEA
Tea Street, @teastreetdenver

CREAMY LEMONADE
Allyson Reedy, @allysoneatsden

PINK DRINK WITH CHOCOLATE COLD FOAM
Lindsay Keosayian, @lindsay.keosayian

ZOMBIE PUNCH
Death & Co, @deathandcompany

SALTED CARAMEL PEAR BOURBON COCKTAIL
Leah Philpott, @leahscucina

SANGRIA SLUSHIE
Lexi Harrison and Beth Sinclair, @crowdedkitchen on TikTok, @crowded_kitchen on IG (crowdedkitchen.com)

RIDICULOUSLY GARNISHED BLOODY MARY
Sobelman's Pub & Grill, @sobelmans

Bubble tea became an "It" drink in Taiwan in the 1980s, but it took throngs of Gen Zers posting photos of their cold, tea-based beverages to make it a global sensation. Besides being pretty to look at—the tea can include fruit chunks, chewy tapioca pearls, milk foam, grass jelly, and more—it's also incredibly tasty and versatile, all of which contributes to the fact that bubble tea shops make up a multibillion-with-a-b-dollar business. (And if you've noticed them popping up in your neighborhood, you're not imagining things—there were just 600 bubble tea shops in the United States in 2015, and now there are well over 5,000.) The best bubble tea spot I know is Denver's Tea Street, and this recipe for lychee mint bubble tea is a must-make. If you're lucky enough to find fresh lychees, use them, but canned work almost as well (and provide the juice you'll need).

HASHTAG PAIRING:
#butfirstlycheetea #bubblehead #spillthetea #grassjellymoney

SERVES 1

LYCHEE MINT BUBBLE TEA

Tea Street | **@teastreetdenver**

2 cups filtered water

2 teaspoons loose-leaf jasmine green tea

1 lime

3 to 4 sprigs mint, plus more for garnish

¼ cup lychee juice from a can of lychees or bottle of juice

Sugar, to taste

Ice, for shaking

3 to 4 fresh peeled lychees or drained canned lychees, diced

1. In a small saucepan, heat the filtered water to 170°F to 180°F. Add the tea and brew for 3 to 5 minutes. Allow to cool.

2. Juice half of the lime and slice the other half to use as a garnish. In a cocktail shaker, muddle the leaves of the 3 to 4 sprigs mint with the lime juice, lychee juice, and sugar.

3. Add ice and pour the cooled tea into the shaker. Shake everything together.

4. Put the diced lychee in a large glass, then pour in the drink.

5. Garnish with lime and mint. Enjoy!

Tinkering with a drink as classic as lemonade is either brilliantly bold or totally stupid. (Come to think of it, "Brilliantly bold or totally stupid" is an excellent tagline for TikTok.) But subbing sweetened condensed milk for the traditional sugar sweetener is definitely brilliantly bold, another of those why-didn't-we-think-of-that-sooner? social media hacks.

Similar to the lime- and sweetened-condensed-milk-filled Brazilian lemonade, another drink that went viral on TikTok, this creamy lemonade drinks exactly as it sounds. Tart and silky, drinking it is almost like sipping lemon meringue pie through a straw, except far less gross than sipping a pie through a straw would actually be.

HASHTAG PAIRING:
#whenlifegivesyoulemons
#stateofthetart
#creamydoesitbetter
#sippingbeyonce

SERVES 4 TO 6

CREAMY LEMONADE

Allyson Reedy | **@allysoneatsden**

1 cup freshly squeezed lemon juice (5 to 6 large lemons)

⅔ to 1 cup sweetened condensed milk

2 cups ice water

Ice, for serving

Lemon slices, for garnish

1. Pour the lemon juice, ⅔ cup sweetened condensed milk, and the water into a small pitcher. Taste and add more sweetened condensed milk, if desired. Stir well. (Seriously, that sweetened condensed milk is thick and needs a good mixing to get it fully incorporated. Feel free to pour the ingredients into a blender, too.)

2. Fill glasses with ice and pour in the lemonade. Garnish with lemon slices and serve with straws.

The Starbucks Pink Drink wasn't supposed to be on the permanent menu. But the Internet fell in love with its pale-pink hue, and even a corporate behemoth like the 'bucks is nothing compared to an army of basic b!tches with Instagram accounts. So, in spring 2017, the company gave in to our viral demands, adding the Pink Lady to its regular roster of six-dollar drinks.

Of course, it helps that the drink also tastes good, especially if you upgrade the strawberry-coconut milk base with chocolate foam. It's like a sippable chocolate-dipped strawberry, resplendent with fruity flavors, a tongue-coating creamy texture, and, yes, an aesthetically pleasing color that's helped it rack up hundreds of thousands of hashtags on the 'gram.

HASHTAG PAIRING:
#pinkdrinkarmy #copycat
#downwithdairy
#onwednesdayswedrinkpink

SERVES 1

PINK DRINK WITH CHOCOLATE COLD FOAM

Lindsay Keosayian | **@lindsay.keosayian**

BASE

1½ cups strawberries

1 cup coconut milk

Ice, for serving

FOAM

¼ cup coconut cream, chilled

1 tablespoon cocoa powder

1 tablespoon maple syrup

Coconut milk, if needed

1. MAKE THE BASE: Chop 2 of the strawberries and set aside. Combine the remaining strawberries and coconut milk in a blender and blitz until smooth.

2. MAKE THE FOAM: In a jar, combine the coconut cream, cocoa powder, and maple syrup and froth with a milk frother or electric whisk until foamy. If the foam is too stiff to pour, thin with coconut milk, adding 1 teaspoon at a time.

3. Fill a tall glass with ice and add the reserved chopped strawberries. Pour in the base, then slowly add the chocolate foam so it remains on top. Add a straw, and enjoy!

The history of this boozy, rum-filled cocktail is a little hazy—gee, I wonder why—but its popularity on social media is crystal clear. (What's not to love about a flaming tiki drink that shares its name with the undead?) Death & Co, the iconic cocktail lair known as one of the world's best bars, ups the rizz factor with fresh pineapple and mint garnish, plus literal sparks flying from the drink. So yeah, you can see why the Internet thinks this drink is total fire. Besides being pretty, the tart lime and grapefruit mixed with warm cinnamon make for a highly sippable zombie.

HASHTAG PAIRING:
#literalfire #itsinyourhead #rumthistowntonight #zombietrendsaintdead

PHOTO TIP: To make sparks fly at home, float an overproof rum into your drink. Light a long match or lighter and set the rum on fire. Quickly sprinkle the flame with ground cinnamon to make it spark. And maybe don't drink before playing with fire.

SERVES 2

ZOMBIE PUNCH

Death & Co | **@deathandcompany**

¼ cup (2 ounces) Don's Mix (recipe follows)

2 ounces light white rum, such as Cana Brava

2 ounces Jamaican rum, such as Smith & Cross

1½ ounces freshly squeezed lime juice

1 ounce falernum

½ ounce grenadine

4 dashes absinthe

2 dashes Angostura bitters

Ice cubes, for shaking and serving

Pineapple fronds, mint leaves, orchids, or whatever you've got on hand, for garnish

2 ounces dark, overproof rum, such as Plantation O.F.T.D.

Ground cinnamon, for flaming

1. Pour the Don's Mix, light rum, Jamaican rum, lime juice, falernum, grenadine, absinthe, and bitters into a cocktail shaker. Add ice and shake for 15 seconds.

2. Strain into ice-filled tall glasses and garnish.

3. Slowly top one drink with 1 ounce of overproof rum. Use a long match to set the rum on fire, then sprinkle cinnamon over the flame to create sparks. Repeat with the other drink.

DON'S MIX

1 cup granulated sugar

3 cinnamon sticks

2½ cups freshly squeezed grapefruit juice (from 3 to 4 grapefruits)

Combine the sugar, 1 cup water, and cinnamon sticks in a small saucepan. Bring to a boil over high heat, then simmer for 10 minutes. Remove from the heat and set aside to rest for 10 additional minutes. Strain into a heatproof jar, discarding the cinnamon sticks, and allow to cool completely. Add the grapefruit juice to the syrup and mix to combine. Cover and keep refrigerated for up to 2 weeks.

I n summer 2023, TikTok gave us girl dinner (soon followed by boy dinner, because *of course*), where users posted snack boards full of rando ingredients and leftovers they ate for their evening meals. While some drinks could potentially be more associated with one sex than the other—*ahem,* Pink Drink—this cocktail is pure gender-neutral sipping bliss. It's rimmed with salted caramel and full of tangy pear-spiked bourbon. Finish it with a strong pour of prosecco and curse the effervescent patriarchy.

HASHTAG PAIRING: #cheers #genderlessdrink #butfirstcocktails #downwithpatriarchy-upwithbourbon

PHOTO TIP: Is it practical to slosh a drink all over the place? Heck no! But does it make for an eye-catching shot? Heck yeah! To really make a splash, drop an ice cube from about a foot above the glass and start snapping.

SERVES 1

SALTED CARAMEL PEAR BOURBON COCKTAIL

Leah Philpott | **@leahscucina**

Caramel sauce and flaky salt, for rim

Ice, for shaking and serving

4 ounces pear nectar

3 ounces bourbon

Juice of 1 orange (about ¼ cup)

Prosecco, for topping

1 thin pear slice and ground cinnamon, for garnish (optional)

1. Grab your favorite cocktail glass, tumbler, or martini glass. Pour a little caramel sauce on a small plate and scatter flaky salt on a separate plate. Dip the rim of the glass in the caramel, and then in the salt. Pop the glass in the freezer while you prepare your drink.

2. Fill a cocktail shaker with ice and pour in the pear nectar, bourbon, and orange juice. Shake for 30 seconds.

3. Fill the chilled glass with ice. Pour the drink over the ice and top with prosecco.

4. If you want to get really fancy, rub the pear slice with the squeezed orange to prevent browning, then sprinkle it with cinnamon and set it on top of the drink.

SANGRIA SLUSHIE

Lexi Harrison and Beth Sinclair | **@crowdedkitchen on TikTok** | **@crowded_kitchen on IG (crowdedkitchen.com)**

I t was the summer of 2016, and frosé was everywhere. It was revolutionary! It was a wine slushie! It was pink! It was, well, actually kind of meh. @crowded kitchen's frozen sangria, made with real fruit and white wine, is a way cooler (oh snap!) take on the wine slushie trend. The mother-daughter @crowdedkitchen team prefers a 50/50 mix of frozen peaches and strawberries, but you could also throw mangoes, cherries, or pineapple into your blender. For the wine, they reach for a Pinot Grigio or Sauv Blanc, but if you have a bottle of Chardonnay lying around, that will work, too.

 # HASHTAG PAIRING:
#nowayfrosé #happyhourhit #frangria #justaddpinot #blendawaytheimpendingdoom

SERVES 3 TO 4

4 cups frozen fruit

2 cups white wine, such as Pinot Grigio or Sauvignon Blanc

¼ cup honey, agave, maple syrup, or another sweetener

Juice of ½ to 1 medium lemon (1 to 2 tablespoons)

Fresh strawberries, for garnish

1. Blend the frozen fruit, white wine, honey, and lemon juice until smooth.

2. Pour into fancy stemware, add a fresh strawberry garnish, and enjoy! (Bonus idea: You can also pour the mixture into a freezer-safe container and freeze it for about 6 hours to make a sangria sorbet, aka the perfect summertime dessert.)

Does anyone really need a cheeseburger slider in their vodka-spiked tomato juice? Probably not, but you might as well put three in your Bloody, plus a skewer of bacon-wrapped steak for good measure. Ridiculously excessive drink garnishes are pretty much a founding pillar of Instagram. They become conversation pieces in and of themselves, and things that you absolutely, positively must take a picture of. Sobelman's Pub & Grill in Milwaukee is known for its, let's just say, quirky Bloody Mary bar, with garnishes ranging from pickled Polish sausages to entire fried chickens. While we'd never want to limit your creativity, here are some adornment ideas that will make you the envy of your horrified followers: baklava, fish sticks, half of a crab, a cheese ball, doughnuts, or an Egg McMuffin.

HASHTAG PAIRING:
#extremebloody
#sundayfunday #moreismore
#sundaybloodysunday
#justaddcheeseball

SERVES 1

RIDICULOUSLY GARNISHED BLOODY MARY

Sobelman's Pub & Grill | **@sobelmans**

8 to 10 ounces tomato juice

2 ounces vodka, such as Tito's

1 scant teaspoon horseradish

3 dashes Worcestershire sauce

1 lime wedge

Kosher salt, to taste

Celery salt, to taste

Ground cayenne pepper, to taste

Freshly ground black pepper, to taste

Ice, for serving

Basic B garnishes, like olives and a celery stalk

Over-the-top garnishes, like a lobster tail, a cheeseburger, and a chicken leg

1. In a cocktail mixing glass or large measuring cup, combine the tomato juice, vodka, horseradish, Worcestershire sauce, and juice from the lime wedge. Season with salt, celery salt, cayenne pepper, and black pepper and use a spoon to stir well.

2. Fill a large glass with ice and pour in the drink. Top with the most depraved garnishes you can muster.

RECOMMENDED READING

D o you love social media cookbooks? Well, obviously! Check out some of our recipe creators' cookbooks for even more viral-worthy recipes.

Complete Air Fryer Series, @flavorsbyfrangipane

Cucina Con Ruben, Ruben Bondi (Cairo)

Death & Co: Modern Classic Cocktails and *Death & Co: Welcome Home*, Alex Day, Nick Fauchald, and David Kaplan (Ten Speed Press)

Drive-Thru Cravings, Calvin Kang

Hardcore Carnivore, Jess Pryles (Agate Surrey)

It's Not Just Cookies, Tiffany Chen and Leon Chen (Harper Horizon)

Love to Eat, Nicole Keshishian Modic (Ten Speed Press)

Memories on a Plate, Carlena Davis

Oh So Tasty and *Oh So Quick and Tasty*, @pollypocketsy

The Salad Lab, Darlene Schrijver (Simon Element)

The Smitten Kitchen Cookbook, *Smitten Kitchen Every Day*, and *Smitten Kitchen Keepers*, Deb Perelman (Knopf)

That's All There Is to It, Carman Wilken

The Ultimate Cookie Handbook, Tessa Arias

The Undrafted Chef (Volumes 1 and 2), Boyd Brown III

The Unofficial TikTok Cookbook, Valentina Mussi (Adams Media)

ACKNOWLEDGMENTS

A huge thank you to all of the social media recipe creators, bloggers, bakers, chefs, and mixologists who provided their amazing recipes. You all are changing the way we eat and drink, and I appreciate your help so much. Thank you for keeping us so well fed!

In addition to her incredible talent and photographs, Chelsea Chorpenning was a fantastic companion throughout this entire process. I cannot imagine the cookbook without her. Her photographs bring this book to life.

My literary agents, Jacklyn Saferstein-Hansen and Alan Nevins, went so far above and beyond typical agent duties. They shaped and encouraged this idea from the get-go, and I am so grateful for you both.

Thank you to everyone at Rizzoli, especially James Muschett, Tricia Levi, and Jessica Napp. Your support, patience,

enthusiasm, and killer editing made this book so much better. So much appreciation for the incredible design by Alison Bloomer, who perfectly captured the book's spirit.

Greg McBoat is my cookbook tribe wrapped up into one spectacular friend, and I couldn't do much of anything without him.

Much love and appreciation to my daughter, Austen, who turned me on to so many of the recipe creators in this book. (And who practiced her Google Sheets skills in the recipe-gathering process.) To her and the rest of my family, who make every day delicious.

INDEX

C

ALLYSON REEDY is a longtime food writer and restaurant critic in Denver, Colorado, and the author of *50 Things to Bake Before You Die* and *30 Breads to Bake Before You Die*. She has written for numerous online and print publications, including *Food52*, *Bon Appétit*, the *Denver Post*, *Thrillist*, and *5280* magazine. When she's not taste-testing or checking out new restaurants for a story, she's probably tripping over her pug in her home kitchen while trying out cookie recipes. Oh, and eating batter and dough by the fistful before her kids ask to lick the bowl; there's a lot of that happening, too.

First published in the United States of America in 2025 by
Rizzoli International Publications, Inc.
49 West 27th Street
New York, NY 10001
www.rizzoliusa.com

Foreword: Snejana Andreeva @themodernnonna
Photography: Chelsea Chorpenning

Publisher: Charles Miers
Associate Publisher: James Muschett
Editor: Tricia Levi
Design: Alison Bloomer
Production Manager: Colin Hough Trapp
Managing Editor: Lynn Scrabis
Copyeditor: Natalie Danford
Proofreader: Sarah Stump

ISBN: 978-0-8478-2978-1
Library of Congress Control Number:
2024946401

FSC
www.fsc.org
MIX
Paper | Supporting
responsible forestry
FSC® C104723

Printed in China
2025 2026 2027 2028 / 10 9 8 7 6 5 4 3 2 1

Visit us online:
Instagram.com/RizzoliBooks
Facebook.com/RizzoliNewYork
X: @Rizzoli_Books
Youtube.com/user/RizzoliNY